T0132278

CHARACTER:
DO YOU HAVE IT?

A Closer Look At Your Relationships

BERNARD POLLARD

BALBOA.PRESS
A DIVISION OF HAY HOUSE

Balboa Press books may be ordered through booksellers or by contacting:

Balboa Press
A Division of Hay House
1663 Liberty Drive
Bloomington, IN 47403
www.balboapress.com
1 (877) 407-4847

Because of the dynamic nature of the Internet, any web addresses or links contained in this book may have changed since publication and may no longer be valid. The views expressed in this work are solely those of the author and do not necessarily reflect the views of the publisher, and the publisher hereby disclaims any responsibility for them.

The author of this book does not dispense medical advice or prescribe the use of any technique as a form of treatment for physical, emotional, or medical problems without the advice of a physician, either directly or indirectly. The intent of the author is only to offer information of a general nature to help you in your quest for emotional and spiritual well-being. In the event you use any of the information in this book for yourself, which is your constitutional right, the author and the publisher assume no responsibility for your actions.

Any people depicted in stock imagery provided by Getty Images are models, and such images are being used for illustrative purposes only. Certain stock imagery © Getty Images.

Print information available on the last page.

ISBN: 978-1-9822-4491-0 (sc)
ISBN: 978-1-9822-4490-3 (hc)
ISBN: 978-1-9822-4492-7 (e)

Library of Congress Control Number: 2020904914

Balboa Press rev. date: 03/11/2020

CONTENTS

INTRODUCTION

I have dedicated my time to helping people understand the relationships in which they encounter throughout life on a daily basis. I have given advice for more than forty years starting with the relationship of my parents and siblings. I have always displayed a passion concerning the insight of individual's personal and relationship problems. This ability to comprehend has aided in the advice which I give to others in understanding the lives that imprison them to fates undesired. If a person could understand the theories which one derives his or her mindset, becomes the suffering of their fate, bringing doom in the end.

Through insightful observation shared in this book one will find functional and dysfunctional foundations which have been laid before us. These, sometimes unwritten guidelines, which are handed down from generation to generation either bury us in or free us from the lives we walk blindly into. Understanding the role which one plays in day to day life is important. If one doesn't know what is to be expected then how will he or she know how to conduct themselves. The information here can and will help individuals to build better relationships once the comprehension of what is expected in life through the character formed throughout that life is put into action. Many may at first reading disagree but once you read and apply the information it becomes easier to accept. I will provide many illustrations for there are several ways character presents itself so good luck in finding yours. One must carefully evaluate his or her own values to obtain the insight that one can stand on what was learned or left to believe and find one's self disagreeing for all the wrong reasons. Now all of that has been said, let's dive into our discussion.

CHAPTER 1

Understanding how the Mindset affects a relationship

Understanding how the Mindset affects a relationship

Let us attempt to understand how the character we possess is formed and then displayed within our lives. It is important to know, because if we do not acquire this knowledge then how do we know how to carry ourselves from day to day. The point here is to bring you to a position of understanding that your character directly affects your daily relationships and it is forever being re-formed depending on who you encounter. It is fair to say "How does one know UP if one has never learned DOWN?" This Theory applies in the same way to one's character. This is the attempt that will be laid out throughout this discussion. Trust and believe everyone is one way or the other and the purpose here is to help everyone figure out which one he or she is and then make the fine tunings as needed.

Does one understand that you walk in multiple forms of relationships in your daily travel through life's journey? Let us examine this point before we move on to the heart of this message. Looking at what role one plays in life is just as important as to knowing how to play that role. This will be discussed in more detail late, but let's take a quick peek. It is fair to say that you are a sister/brother, mother/father, aunt/uncle, niece/nephew, husband/wife, boyfriend/girlfriend, cousin/co-worker, parent/child, and finally friend/enemy. Unless you are special, you are born or procreate into these positions, but you have to learn your role through developing your character. Try this illustration out to get the mind going. Now imagine being born into a situation where two sisters constantly feud. Now imagine what aunt/cousin relationship that you will have based on your mother developing your behavior toward that particular family group.

What happens to the relationship before it can develop is where the unseen catastrophe is taking place. The sister's do not get along so they never properly introduce the children which are blood cousins. The children in return cannot build a relationship of respect toward the aunt or the cousins. This will make it hard despite their personal efforts in building their own characters in life to maintain the balance if any discord takes place with people they are related to but don't know. Starting to get the picture?

That is why we must understand that people judge your character by your outward expressions. One must understand character is derived from an inward buildup of personality. Many teachings have accepted what is called The Big Five Factors or O.C.E.A.N.

The Five Factors are:

1. **O**penness is appreciation for a variety of experience
2. **C**onscientiousness is planning ahead rather than being spontaneous
3. **E**xtraversion involve going out with friend and being energetic

4. **A**greeableness is, as it says, being agreeable
5. **N**euroticism refers to worrying or being vulnerable

Think about it, no one would know if you are considerate unless you first show it in your actions. I don't want to get to deep on this yet, but we will come back to this subject later.

Understanding how our mindset affects our relationship is the first thing that we need to know. This is key for it is through the mind that every key message of personality is conveyed to the outside world. This is why it is important to understand that there is basically two ways to live your life FUNCTIONALLY and DYSFUNCTIONALLY and that was decided long ago at the tree in the garden. Let us examine the points carefully in order to understand where we may fall.

We will first examine functional behavior. Functional Behavior is typically developed from a standard that exist about life and the way to live it. When we expect something to function correctly, we look for positive outcomes. It would be foolish to put one's hard earned money into a CD, IRA, or some form of investment plan if a substantial amount of interest is not expected in the long run, right. Then one must ask themselves, when it comes to the lives that we live why do we demean people that would seem to represent the meaning of a functional lifestyle more so than what we are used to seeing.

The answer is simple, when one looks beyond the box that he or she is used to living in, all things looks strange. We tend to find negative expressions about these things rather than seek the knowledge to understand them. This becomes simple to understand if one can accept this analogy: ***The eyes are the binoculars to world we see, analyzing information brought in by the foreknowledge inputted into the brain.*** To clear up those that may have gotten lost there for that was deep. If you are raised in a community where people cuss each other rather they are getting along or not, then one might think it strange when meeting someone that does not cuss, fair to say? Now let's move on.

Over the next few pages we will talk about functional behavior and give illustrations to help you to understand how it works and where you may fall concerning this matter.

Functional Character

Being functional allows us to miss those bumps in the road that otherwise leads to the turbulence that many experience. A good foundation starts from a well thought out plan. I often say *"Nobody Plans to Fail, They Just Fail to Plan."* This is so true starting from our childbirth. Take a look at our parent's lifestyle at the time of our conception. If your parents would fall under the functional standpoint, planning the marriage, securing stable employment, providing the home, marrying and then having children do you think that this would have possibly changed your outlook on life.

Why of course it would, and that my friend is called structure the beginning of building one's character. We must understand that what you do in building your character is based on pre-set values in your life rather you can put your finger on them or not, they are there. The more things in your life that have structure then the less things in your life that you tend to worry about. That is the formula to well- rounded character. Example: A man learns the value of hard work as a child and carries those surrounding principles into his adult life. He works hard, saving his money and meets the right woman in his eyes and plans to marry her, buys a house and plans for the arrival of his children.

It would be a clear assumption to make that if all goes as

planned (for this illustration) as his children come into the world, he should be able to keep up with life's untimely events. Many believe to have a setback in life is to completely fall apart, not true, for even a well-functioning vehicle needs an oil change. A functional well-planned life works the same way, after all you do not pay insurance so you can get in an accident but rather for if you get into one. Yet, how many of us follow the functional plan for years concerning insurance payments only to never get into an accident. What's funny is we brag about not getting into the accident never focusing on all the money paid along the way. The money spent can never be recovered but it protected us along the way.

Life should be looked at the same way for all purposes and intent. One should always secure a plan to communicate despite the problems one may encounter. Likewise, communication is like the money one spends which sees relationships through the arguments (accidents) along the way, maintaining the bond we do not want o lose. It is the downfalls as well as bad information given to us along the way of life's journey that prevents us from communicating. Understand it is through constant communication we salvage broken relationships. It is through constant communication that prevent relationships from breaking. See how things that are taught can help or hinder the thinking processes that are there to build the character one walks in, only to strengthen the relationships we build.

When we look at common practices within our daily lives you will be surprised how they help others to determine our character. Hold on, what did he just say? When you meet someone that is hard working, loving/kind, sharing, responsible, and respectful we don't realize how much time that someone put into that person in their developmental years. We admire that person and brag on their character but not really understanding how they got there. Well let's take a look.

Starting with Hard Work it most likely was forged within the early ages of 4-5 years old when his parents taught him/her how to pick up behind themselves thus giving them their first chore and staying consistent throughout the years. These others are added into the forming of one's character from there;

- Loving/kindness they are taught through "charity starts in the home" how you treat your sister/mother is most likely how you will treat your wife.
- Treat others as you would like to be treated. (Be careful you have to show them the right way before you turn them loose on this one).
- Sharing is something that allows you to interact with others from a compassionate standpoint. This takes time to develop, lots of time.
- Responsible is what you become when you accept the teachings of hard work and the ethics of life. This takes time.
- Respect is to know how to conduct yourself with others when you are happy with them and even more so when you are in disagreement with them.
- How can a Lady look forward to being treated like a Queen if a father never treated her like a Princess?
- How can a man walk in the steps of a King if a father never showed him how to walk as a Prince?

Anyone can show good character when things are going their way, but I challenge you to maintain good character when they are not. Now listen to the difference of how people see you from a well rounded standpoint.

One should start to see that Character is one word that is brought together by several different viewpoints in your life. That is why it so important to understand how the perception that we give based on the teachings that we have underwent in life are so important to the daily relationships that we are involved in. One must understand that your (outward) attitude is the expression of your (inward) character. I laugh when people with a bad attitude say "you don't know me" and I think to myself it is you that has not met the real you yet.

It is fair to say that when you have been taught from a functional standpoint, one tends to put out a positive perception which in return reaps positive rewards. I mentioned earlier that good character allows you to miss bumps in life, let us look at some examples.

1. When you are taught to return what you borrow. You don't fall out with people
2. When you are polite with all. You don't usually get snappy remarks in return.
3. When you learn to wait your turn to speak. You don't argue so often.
4. Don't accuse without supporting evidence. You are not always apologizing.
5. If you want to be trusted. Show yourself to be trustworthy. (Worthy of one's trust)

There are several others that you may find as you examine your own lives now that you are seeing the pattern.

I don't want you to misunderstand by thinking if you have a lifestyle that is predominately functional that adversity won't rise against you. This is the furthest thing from the truth as can be told. What I am merely saying is that when you have structure (function) people will always come and challenge you to see if it is real. Yet hold to your standards and you will overcome their efforts to bring you down. A well-woven rope is not easy to break. When your character is woven together by many strong personality traits it is hard for people to knock you down though sometimes, we are shaken.

Function is the way of life that is set by the standards of life, remember that and your problems will be few. Understanding standards and their purpose is the key to developing a structure leading to good character as you interact with people throughout life. This is something key to remember: *Understand everything and now accept that which you understand then little will ever surprise you.* There is so much meaning to this statement that if you think too hard about it you will miss the meaning.

This is key to the development of your character because one does not need to agree with everything people say, but one does need to understand everything that people speak. Many get caught up on proving to others they do not agree with what was spoken when all that is really needed is to understand why they spoke it. Now accept what you just learned and you will know how to deal with them each time you speak to them from that day forward. The recipe has always been out there but our eyes can only pull in the information leaving the brain to process it by the foundational knowledge we have been exposed to.

Functional people don't settle for bad outcomes, but rather they are of the proactive nature so they continue to develop new ways to not repeat bad behavior. People that are functional are used to a sense of peaceful living in their daily lives. This is why they continue to refine the standards in which they live by to achieve perfect peace in their relationship. Function in a positive way is the long-term goal not necessarily the every time you interact outcome. Many get lost here for they want to believe every encounter has to be a positive one so we make delusional phrases to fit the delusion.

Have many of you heard "Let's agree to disagree?" I have met many people that have attempted to convince me this makes sense. I keep telling people it doesn't when you look at things from a functionally logical position. Well let's examine the next scenario to see if there is any truth to what is stated here. Remember this first that for something to be taken in as a standard to build one's character on it would be nice if it is full proof. Simply saying that the advice should get you through just about any situation. Here we go.

- John and Larry have been working together for about 10 years in the same department. They normally talk to each other about small issues of life, sporting events, and vacations, etc. One day John finally approaches Larry about borrowing $10 on September 1st and will give it back on the 30th of the month. Larry looks at the years of acquaintance and gladly agrees to the terms. John ask him for the same favor the following week with the payback date remaining the same. This pattern happens on the following two weeks, yet the payback date remaining the same. When the 30th arrives John gives Larry the $10 that he borrowed with a smile of appreciation. Larry says to John "hey you borrowed $40 from me" and John responds "I never borrow more than $10." Larry say "you didn't borrow more than $10 at a time but you borrowed $10 on the 1st, 8th, 15th, and the 22nd, coming to a grand total of $40." John (who loses track because he borrows from so many people) says "here's $20 for the confusion but let's just *agree to disagree*. Larry is livid and tells John to never speak to him again.

Is it clear how you cannot *agree to disagree* because then you are only being less than who you are by continuing to interact with a person like John? Mark Twain wrote "The problem with arguing with a fool is the onlookers soon forget who the fool is." John gets over for he never pays the amount he borrowed and Larry would have to overlook his losses to continue a relationship with John. Many of us do just that on a daily basis and cannot figure out why we argue so much within these forms of relationships. I know some of you may still be thinking, not me, so let's look a little deeper.

The reason people accept this saying is because they have learned to converse in this manner. Using an illustration with siblings seems to work well for this portion. How many of us with siblings have argued about something and you know that you are correct on the issue? The parent has just arrived home not long ago and doesn't want to hear what he or she categorizes as noise and tells both children to quiet down. This happens more often than what you may realize. So, you are thinking right about now "what should have happened?"

Before I tell you how this should have went let me tell you why it should not have gone that way. First, I am going to give the scenario life to make it better to understand. Child number one was watching television and child number two came in from outside and decided to claim the television because he or she is oldest. Child number one has a legitimate complaint to why the issue exists but the parent simply tells both children to turn the television off and to be quiet. Both children are left to learn that when you do not agree just simply let it go, agree to disagree.

The child which is right losses out on the privileges of life which reward you with a peace of mind for doing things the right way. While the child that is wrong (for this illustration) never learns what is wrong with his or her behavior. This child is more apt to use the phrase, agree to disagree, because it keeps a person from being accountable for his or her actions. Just as there is a sense of pride for being right there is also a sense of pride in manipulation for those that travel this road. It is important for the parent to sit the children down to sort out the problem so pride is built in a positive way for it will come up again in the future.

Many have a hard time understanding the issues they face in their adult life within the relationships they dwell. The reason people are able to communicate is so they may resolve, for this is the intention. The scenario above cripples the knowledge to be learned and this is why so many problems exist within relationships. So, it becomes common to "agree to disagree" never resolving one's issues leaving us to dwell in misery. The problem left to live with now is breaking the bad habits to get back to where we should be so we can learn the proper methods or standards of life.

- Virginia was raised to wait until acknowledged to speak by her parents. This teaching has allowed her to get along with her teachers from the time she entered school. Virginia learns many things in life because the etiquette of communicating instilled helps her to understand life and then apply those learnings as needed to her own life. Now Jack has parents that are proud his vocabulary is expanded for a child his age (2) and allows him to openly express. Between the ages of 2-5 Jack learns to speak to people to the point he basically dominates conversations. This goes unnoticed until Jack enters kindergarten and the complaints roll in. Teachers throughout his school years do not like him in their class though he is a smart student. Jack builds a spiteful attitude towards his authority. This attitude Jack has found himself harboring keeps him from receiving essential information that will help him later in life. Now as life sometimes happens for us, Virginia is on a head on collision to meeting Jack. Both students are on the honor roll and plan on attending college. They meet in their senior year of high school and date throughout college. Jack is a great talker so Virginia finds herself listening to him even when they disagree but he talks over her to settle the issue. They eventually marry and have children and all seems to go well for the two. Jack thrives in working and provides for his children but Virginia is starting to believe Jack doesn't hear her when she says she could use a hand around the home. Jack does tell her that everything will be alright (which is at the least an acknowledgement of her request) but shows no follow-through. As the years pass and the children grow out of the home Virginia shows great signs of depression with the marriage and Jack suggest counseling, for her. The counselor talks to Virginia and encourages her to open-up about her deep seeded issues. It comes to light that Jack loves to tell you what you can do but he never seems to put himself in the picture or hear your suggestions. The counselors request Jack comes to at least one of the sessions so he can get an impression of his character and Jack politely agrees. During the session Jack tells the counselor all about how Virginia allows things to get to her and she just needs to be tougher. When the conversation attempts to turn to Jack he dismisses it with he provides for his family and the children are all in college prepping for the next phase of life. The counselor ends the session. Now I challenge many of you reading this to try and understand what has happened here. I am going to help you, as many of you knew I would.

Jack	Virginia
1. Jack learned to talk but not listen	1. Virginia learned to respect authority
2. Jack learned to take control	2. Virginia stood down when the issues become heated
3. Jack learned self-confidence	3. Virginia over-time developed low self-esteem
4. Jack became blind to his ways and other's needs	4. Virginia became depressed
5. Jack's character became hardened	5. Virginia's character became brittle and shattered

Are you starting to get it with Jack and Virginia how their lives had similarities which made them look like the perfect couple. Yet the differences in their up-bringing changed the way it all played out. Many of us experience this example but we say the person changed because we fail to recognize what took place before we ever met the individual. The real problem here is many of us never learn how to deal with these issues even after we recognize them. As I have said many of times "the teachings instilled will guide the character of one's personality in which people see" and you will find this to be true.

This brings me to another point to build on while I am on this subject, "character trait-vs-quality trait." Many of us confuse quality and character traits for they are very similar yet not exactly the same. Your character is defined by the morals and ethics instilled and the quality of this is displayed as the role is fulfilled. Allow me to present another illustration to give little visual.

- Roy is raised by his mother and father who are happily married and they have three other children. Roy was taught to do what his mother and father told him and followed a regular routine on a daily basis. He was taught to cover his mouth when he coughs or sneezes for this is a form of respect for others. Roy was taught to be patient and wait for the right time to interject his views in a conversation so others may not get frustrated. The point here is Roy was taught the ethical way to treat people to yield positive results. Here if one would continue to walk with Roy throughout his life those traits he was taught ethically will determine what he has learned and then display (i.e., morals and ethics---character traits---quality traits). I want you to see how this works. It is the moral and ethical value of learning not to become *anxious when speaking* allowing the character of *patience* to show therefore making people desire to be around Roy because his quality trait is not *argumentative*.

If people would apply this theory or standard to their daily behavior to determine how they have become who they are, there would be the need for major changes in our lives. By no means am I saying someone is a bad person but I am saying if we build our character on sound principles then we all could be better than what we are. It is important to know people judge us by the character we display, not for the one we wish to be.

Dysfunctional Character

Now let us examine the problems with a Dysfunctional way of life and how character falls into it. Many have become blind to the way he or she is and cannot understand why he or she deals with the problems gained during interaction with others. When you live a life that has no foundation based on little standards this will explain why your life may be so sporadic. Now this is not to say there is no foundation but merely to imply the foundation consist of the wrong materials that cannot support a positive outcome.

Sit back and prepare yourself because many of us can relate to our character under this clause, but as I point out these things that may pertain to your life, don't slip into denial because that only allows you to cut off the help that is much needed. As we have seen in the functional realm the stability that bonds two people together, that is what we won't see in this realm because dysfunction only drives us apart. People say things like: "There is no perfect relationship" only to not understand that a chaotic relationship is still not the answer.

I have told people I would rather go through one hour of hell in Heaven rather than one hour of peace in Hell. You may not be the only one stumped by this quote, so allow me to explain. An hour of good or bad should not define a relationship when there are twenty-three more hours in a day. The irony here is the success of any relationship resides in how two people spend the majority of their time, not one hour. The scary part is people live out what they know and it is fair to say if they have not learned much then they will not live much.

I have talked with so many couples that do not have a clue about where they are and especially how they got there. These are the couples I refer to as "Granite Couples" for it will take time to get them to unlearn and then relearn so they may enjoy true happiness for once. Before I move on I have to share with you this tidbit about the belief many couples have.

Many couples refer to their relationship in comparison to the Cinderella story and I smile because I know they do not realize the truth in which they speak. I always ask them to tell me about the comparison they see and this is how it normally goes:

> I was doing badly in life because my parents were never together or things were rough because money was tight. I met my husband and he swept me off my feet. We instantly fell in love for he was my knight in shining armor as the Prince to Cinderella in the fairy tale. I now ask so everything is peachy now that you started your family? She politely answers "No, for there is no perfect relationship. I now ask can I speak to maybe shed more light on the issue. I get the response "by all means."
>
> This is why many relationships fall under the umbrella of the Cinderella story. Many people start off in life with money being an issue during their childhood years. Many women believe they meet the man of their dreams because he has a good job but cannot for the life of them see how their life could possibly line up to Cinderella. When Cinderella married the Prince the story says she lived Happily Ever After, or did she? Most couples don't so why would we buy in that Cinderella did. Look deeper at the "ever after part" and now remember the stories behind women

who marry men of wealth and it should start to clear your thoughts.

Men of power and wealth typically enjoy the pick of the bunch when it comes to women. Kings and Princes have had several concubines the Queen had to deal with or overlook, if you will. Now if you are arguing about "the other woman" and your man provides a nice living but women are making themselves known to him, NOW you are living the Cinderella Story.

My reason for pointing this out is to show how one has adapted dysfunction into the lives he or she lives and call it normal or happy. If this applies to you or someone you know then pay close attention as we talk about the shaping of character in and throughout our relationships.

Getting back to where I left off. If we look at the same scenario of childbirth, but from the dysfunctional position we can now start to see why our lives are in such disarray. If your parents started having sex and unfortunately you are conceived so they marry. Moms on welfare and dad can't find a job for various reasons; imagine the financial hardships and arguments that take place in your life during your developmental years.

I believe also that when a parent's life is full of argument then they don't have time to teach standard or develop structure. We accept clichés that really have been established under the mindset of dysfunction. See if you can recall some of these;

- Opposites attract
- Nothing like make-up sex
- Argument makes your relationship stronger
- Give a person their space

- We all have a person that we can rely on (other than the one you're with)
- Family comes first
- Blood is thicker than water
- He is a jack of all trades

These are but only a few that you have heard. Let us attempt to understand why these clichés are not good for you to walk by.

1. Opposites attract is good for magnets but not humans. When you are around anyone whose character isn't compatible to yours it is only a matter of time before you are at each other's throat. Imagine a girl chooses a guy because he is everything she is not. He goes out, he drinks and seems fun, and he knows a lot of people, and so on. It is a given that after about a year or two into the relationship these become the very reasons they argue. He is always gone, he drinks too much, and people are always calling or coming by.

2. If you are always enjoying make up sex, ask yourself how long you will keep tolerating the argument that led to the sex. Why do people destroy their daily interaction with their mate to hope to enjoy a once a week romp in the sheets? Do the math and you will come to the same answer as myself, "it is only a matter of time to breakup."

3. Keep arguing and watch how you sit further apart on the couch when you watch a movie or how you can't remember the last time that you had a civil conversation. The relationship has faded but couples are now living in formality so all of the quality is gone and routine has taken over.

4. If you never learn how to talk through the bad times, you will soon just stop talking. People ask for their space when there has been a disagreement, but resolutions can only be found by continuing to communicate. I know many of you are thinking "I just need time" and you are fooling yourself. Count how many times when you used the "give me space" clause, you came back and talked about it or simply dismissed the issue because we are no longer arguing.

5. Number 4 helps us to understand why we talk to someone else except our mate. Here we find what is called a "substitute" because we really want to talk but anger prevents us from talking to the one we love. We therefore find a substitute, normally of the opposite sex or the same sex of our partner. Look at it like this, a teacher calls in sick so the school fills in with a substitute. Though someone else is teaching the class for the day the job still belongs to the absent teacher. Couples operate under the same manner, you temporarily stop talking to your mate only to find someone else to vent to. Notice you remain with the mate as a couple but you are talking more to the substitute.

6. If your mate is not above your family ties then you may as well date your family. People will quickly say "nothing comes before family" well yes it does, FAMILY. There are two levels of family, the one you are born into and the one you marry into for procreation. It seems that people don't date to start a family but simply for pleasure and this is why we never establish the mentality needed to successfully carry out this unwritten rule. We seek people to have sex with and then just remain together calling it family because the outcome looks synonymous. Imagine

if while dating, before sex, we asked family questions such as; how many children do you desire? What role as a man/woman do you see yourself playing in a family setting? What is the plan to resolving our differences as they arise? This line of communication before sex will save you a lot of headache down the line.

7. This directly points to mate vs family. Spill a glass of blood and a glass of water and tell me which one stains. Simply put, born in family knows your life and is willing to tell it from the anger of struggle or vindictiveness from growing up. Your mate takes a vow of "honor" when you marry to hold your secrets or short comings. In short, blood (born family) exposes and water (procreation family) cleanses through resolution.

8. Women love to label their man as a "jack of all trades" but not realizing the origin of this statement describes a man that is very average or completes very little. The next time you hear the statement listen for the follow-up of what he brings to the relationship. Normally he is not gainfully employed or minimal income, he can't commit to a relationship, he may be good in the bed (all the energy from not working), he participates in the start of a conversation but bails when it get to a boiling point, and etc. This is what the completion of the quote is telling you, "Jack of all trades, yet the master of none."

Sometimes we never question where some of these clichés that we so readily accept derive from, but by the same token we don't understand how our lives end up the way they are. One doesn't understand it is the information instilled forging the lives one lives, creating the success or failures we endure.

If you take the principles of algebra you can see how it will support my theory.

- Negative and a negative equal a negative
- Negative and a positive equal a negative
- Positive and a positive equal a positive, Stop and Listen

Life works the same way; two negative people will possibly never achieve true happiness together for the problems they will create. Lives such as this falter because of the issues both parties bring to the table and then they walk a life of tolerance. Tolerating each other, never finding true happiness, possibly waiting on the other to die.

A negative and positive will settle for spurts of good times trying to overlook all the bad ones. Remember earlier I stated about living one hour of peace in Hell, this is what many relationships reflect. The characters here are so different people spend their energy attempting to change the other. If they desire to remain together, they simply co-exist looking for the 1-week vacation to get away and return for fifty-one weeks tolerating the other until the next vacation.

Two positive people will forge paths together no matter what their relationship status because the more you have in common toward the good the less you clash. The formula here is so full proof that it can't be denied no matter who you are and how you try. People need to understand the ability to communicate and resolve is the foundation to any relationship because issues don't build. It is the compounding of issues unresolved that keeps the past in the present.

In the dysfunctional world we quickly distance ourselves from those that seem to stand out functionally. Let's take a look at some examples; When we drink, we think it weird to meet someone that has never drank alcohol before. When I went into the military my childhood associates

We encourage bad behavior, rather than be proud of someone for being good. This can normally be found when people down you by calling names like "goody two shoes" and many others. This tends to be a default mechanism found in human behavior when something happens outside of our daily norm. People who rarely stay home will call a homebody "boring" without first understanding what activities are done in the home that are exciting.

We develop our lives a certain way and then we find others that think like we do and that becomes our social existence. If one would take the time to really determine if they are living under the functional or dysfunctional realm of life, this would make things simple. You must first be honest with yourself about yourself and the company that you keep. Remember the saying: "birds of a feather flock together." Let's take a look at the way character is played out here.

Try and list the standards that you walk by and see if your friends walk by the same standards. For argument sake I will list a few and you at home can complete the list pertaining to your lives. To give you a better understanding I will list three categories; the trait and the two ways it can be taken. Here goes.

Trait	Person1	Person2
drinker	casual	drunk
smoker	casual	chimney
partier	occasional	life of the party
movie watcher	seeks clarity	got through it
conversationalist	resolver	opinionated

Being functional allows us to miss those bumps in the road that only cause turbulence in the lives that we live. If we take the time to first be honest with ourselves about which category that we fall in then we can start this journey to a better relationship. The dysfunctional relationship is compounded when we mix and match the above traits but are fooled by the titles of similarity.

Take a closer look at the drinker. Two drinkers may meet at a club, bar, or friendship acquaintance. The two talk over a drink but if one is not careful it can be quickly assumed the other drinks in the common manner as he or she does. Time goes on and the place of residence becomes the same location and now the eyes are opened to more of the person's ways. The argument is about the drinking but the drunk stands his or her ground stating "you knew I drank when you met me" but not to this degree.

Look at the smokers now. It would almost seem there could be little problem here because they both smoke, big deal. The casual smoker may not smoke in the home or the car but the chimney smoker lights up at the slightest opportunity. When people first meet the depth of one's displayed behavior should be 80 % of the conversation setting the stage. This can become one of the main channels for arguing.

The partier is where most couples meet and the reason the relationship falls apart. Some people go out casually and most people go out like working a job, with perks. The occasional partier's life set around responsibility and a party is penciled in when convenient. The "life of the party" individual is committed to fun and will miss work or take frivolous jobs in order to not miss "the happenings." The differences normally surface when the female has a baby, secures a home, or is met with some sense of responsibility.

Movie watching is tricky because almost everyone will swear

by it that they like to watch movies. If one does not think about it carefully one may never connect with the intent of the plot the producer is attempting to convey. Movies and books are written to indirectly convey messages which many people miss. This is where understanding the reason why a person watches a movie is important because it can differ from the reason you may watch them. Some people watch movies because it challenges their reasoning faculties in figuring things out. This is a self-fulfilling moment for them so they attempt to share with others the plots and turns of the writer. Now there are those who watch movies because they are made to (school, family time, just to get close to the person, and so on) and this is why there is a clash between these two styles. If a person is wondering why the two of them argue when attempting to speak on a movie after it is over, this could be the reason.

Conversation works the same way. Conversation is designed to resolve the issues which come about within our lives. This is why I have heard so many people say they enjoy just living with their pets (cats, dogs, birds, etc.) and they can talk to them and gain a sense of composure. This is farther from the truth than many realize. A pet cannot speak back so one is left to interpret the pet's actions favorably to what they want to hear. The person who uses conversation the way it is supposed to be used is only attempting to build bonds to strengthen the relationship, but the conflict comes into play when speaking to a person who does not regard conversating the same way.

CHAPTER 2

Understanding the role that you play in a relationship

The next step that we have to undertake is getting people to understand the role that they play in their relationship. It is important for us to realize that if we don't understand our role and heaven forbid that the other person doesn't understand theirs either, what mess do we leave ourselves to live in.

To be able to live any role in life I believe that you must first understand what you are getting into by knowing the full attributes of the role you portray.

Let us look at a few roles so we together can come to a better conclusion of the main roles we play in life contributing to our character. Remember I said earlier in the opening of the book about roles. It is fair to say that you are a sister/brother, mother/father, aunt/uncle, niece/nephew, husband/wife, boyfriend/girlfriend, cousin/co-worker, parent/child, and finally friend/enemy.

If one should examine the common factors which exist among these roles it is interesting how they lend to the perception one views in our character. What a person learns in each of these roles can make or break them as they enter into the more stable times of their life. The complexity in understanding these roles is because there are times when one inherits multiple roles at once. So, it can be challenging if there is not a clear understanding of the roles and how they intertwine. Let's point outa few things about each set in which I have laid out.

Sister/brother: As a child it clearly takes at least two children to fulfill this role. Yet one has to be taught how to respect, share, and consider the belongings of another. It is in this stage the foundation of relationships is taught that can carry you through the most important roles ahead. Learning to respect is important because a role parallel to this will show up again in your future as a mate. One must understand that the properties of respect develops from the qualities, abilities, and accomplishments of the other person. This is why it is important to teach a child to focus (train) on their sibling this skill because it can save him or her many headaches from choosing the wrong mate down the line. When respect is properly applied then sharing and consideration simply falls into place.

Mother/father and parent/child: I will blend these together for they make up the family structure. The mother and father have to have ground rules that stabilize the way they will run the home. This is important for a parent can spend time with the child(ren) and this could allow manipulation by that child to come in between the parents. This is why a good example would be: The mother is home with the children all day and the father is employed to provide for the family. The child(ren) are conditioned to mom being the daily disciplinarian and instructor of the household rules. If the child is told no to something and comes to realize the father is not aware, for he is at work, then the child would catch the father coming in the door and ask for what he or she knows they were told no about. The way this should be handled is the father should refer back to the agreement with mom and say "let me check with your mother" and this will stop manipulation while serving a dual purpose to building a stronger bond between the parents. This also sends a signal to the child that the parents together have authority over the child(ren) in the household and that bond will not be broken. Manipulation by children is normal, but the problems exist when the adults do not stand in unity (through previous discussion) of the expected things to happen.

Aunt/uncle: This role gets tricky because one can take on this role because of an older sibling who has a child while you are only ten years old. The problem is that the child is trying to figure out how he or she should act, but has to build a future respect for this role with a child they have come to know under a childish mentality. Pertaining to the grownup in this role, he or she has to remember to not make your niece or nephew the extension of the unresolved issues between you and your sibling. Many people do not understand how they destroy family bonds by bringing the next generation into unresolved issues of their own childhood. What must be understood here is the dynamics which happened when one was 12 through 18 years of age are hard for the next generation to comprehend because of the many advancements in society. Look at the fights over watching the one television in a home with six family members in the 70s and 80s compared to now there is a television in every room. This only destroys the respect of many of the roles in which we speak about today. Remember also to not treat your siblings' children differently because they are not your children.

Niece/nephew: Though this role can be hard to fulfill for many people don't have where they see their aunts and uncles on a daily basis. The issues here are hopefully minimized because if a child is taught to respect all adults then that should cover most issues.

Husband/wife: This role weighs in the most for there is a great deal of understanding that goes into this. One must first understand that every role mentioned is one that a person is born into, inherit by taking employment, or develop because you are a good or bad person. This role is the most important of any of them for this is the only role that a person signs a lifetime contract to fulfill. I know many of you parents out there take on a marriage (sometimes it is not to the biological parent of the child) but the contract does not change. The husband and wife role are **leaving mother and father and forsaking all others (all roles mentioned)** to build the bond that will allow them to stay together until death do you part. I know many parents say that nobody comes before my child only to find themselves living in broken relationships to face the fact of the child leaving you based on the statement in bold. In today's society there are many blended families, families which are built from previous relationships of the man and woman before coming together as one, (Merriam-Webster, 2019). It appears to be because of this, the focus of this role is lost in the shuffle of the ex (on both sides) having say about the authority of the home, disguised as concern for the children. Children will catch on quick to this and turn the parents against each other to gain an advantage. If the two people understand what they are getting into and stay strong to the contract this can override any attempts to foil the life-time commitment. It is through this role that talking about what future endeavors are to be accomplished with bringing two or more families together is important. There are so many dynamics and voices to be heard in the blended family setting leading to why this relationship can be easily derailed. This is why planning must be as close to perfect as possible for it to work.

Boyfriend/girlfriend: This is another tricky one because the distortion here goes deep. The true meaning for the boyfriend/

girlfriend role is to find the one to whom you wish to live the rest of your life with. I had the pleasure of hearing many people dispute how there is nothing wrong with dating as a child. I love the challenge of this statement so I ask can I run a few things pass you and they agree. I first set the tone for a male about 35 years of age, working a part-time job, and doesn't help with much of the home chores and children. Woman will leap on how he is no good and she can do bad all by herself. I normally allow her to get the rant out of her system before I continue, because I need her to hear what I am about to say. I continue by asking her where does she think he developed this behavior. Most respond with probably a lazy father or a missing father, I laugh usually. I tell her this behavior is developed from parents that are too liberal with freedoms by not knowing how to wing a child into the life ahead of them. This boy and girl are allowed to date with no guidance to avoid the traps (opportunities) which bring about sex leading to teen pregnancy. The first missed deception is the two of them dating to the full-term of the word for they are not in the position to marry at this time let alone raise a family. Yet if a boy is dating at 12 years of age then his parent(s) is/are giving him the money, giving him a ride to the dating site, and helping him to create his grand delusion. I know many of you are thinking "what delusion" and I am about to tell you. The delusion that the adult woman has to deal with in the reality of life as in;

1. He won't commit to a job to cover life's expenses
2. He expects her to do the greater share for the family
3. He may have his hand out for money
4. He still hangs out with his friends until late into the night

Many parents don't want to accept this for there is always the exception to the rule, but not that many exceptions, so we need to own it. This is why if the child is allowed to date it must come with restrictions as to not allow a dimension of adulthood to set in while in the dimension of childhood, for 12 to 17-year-old people are normally not looking for husbands and wives. So, to understand that 35-year-old male, he is only seeing the partner as he saw his parents, give me everything though I have worked for nothing.

Cousin/co-worker: This is similar to the aunt/uncle role for if you don't see your cousin on a daily basis and you don't live with your co-worker then the roles can be confusing. With cousin and co-worker there is that sense of family, but there are times we forget the respecting factors which comes with it. Cousins should not be in a position to prove that each other are liars, cheats, and many other things, because in family one should be honest and upfront with one another. Co-workers have similarities through a form of brotherhood or some allegiance. This is clearly seen in law enforcement, military, sports, and so on where a sense of loyalty is expected. When the proper respect, consideration, and trust is applied the roles are bonded. The thing to understand here is that in most of these situations the bonds are built after the first eighteen years of life, not during, which can cause a strain.

Friend/enemy: The role of a friend is questionable for many of us make a friend only to discover an enemy (**frienemy**). This normally happens if one definitely has not done well at many of the other roles. Have you ever met a person that will tell you all of their business the first week of meeting you? Have you ever met a person that will ask you personal questions about yourself in the first week of meeting you? You may well be on your way to finding a frienemy. Understand that people that don't follow a respectable path will gossip, backstab, lie, manipulate, and so on to get what they want or to get where they are going.

Most people will come with the mentality of a child and not realize it. Do you remember when you were a child or when your child went to his or her first day of kindergarten? Most children come home and tell you they made 12 friends today, remember now? You come to find out that is the number of how many people are in their class. Some people never grow out of that mentality and suffer throughout life because of it. It is this mentality which allows us to make instant friends at work, church, new neighborhoods, and the biggest one Facebook. A person opens their life up to people because they are suffering from the inability of forming positive roles in their life, only to be hurt by the betrayal of those they confided in.

Do you understand now how if one doe not understand the roles in their life it can topple every role like dominoes in your life, leaving you without answers to the questions which bury you. This is why it is important to master the attributes of these roles, building a strong character so you can face life as a champion in this battle. Let me give you a few examples of how a frienemy will slip into your life unaware to your defenses.

When we learn to talk as a child it is easy to say everything about anything that happened in front of you. This is why one may come to understand, if you don't want something known then don't do or say it in front of a child, and this is true. Children have to learn how to build a filter in what is proper to say and what is not. How many kids are embarrassed because the school found out all their parents do is argue, but the truth is the child told another child who told everybody else. So, it is fair to say the child brought the house down on themselves.

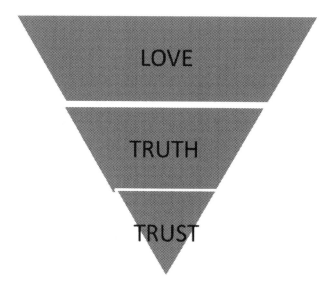

CHAPTER 3

Truth, trust, and love: The role they play

This chapter is one of my favorite subjects for there is a lot of meaning in this subject. Many people never come to the understanding that many words are process words. This means there is a process at work within the word itself which one must fulfill to get the best outcome from using the word. As we take this journey to understanding how character is developed in connection to using these words one can make the necessary changes, for it is never too late. One of the biggest deterrents for people is the ever-evolving usage of words within our social setting. I use the term "back yard bar-b-que setting" to describe the social gathering where people sit around to exchange their opinions and at the least any advice. This becomes the norm for people so much information is lost or never gained which could turn their lives around in a positive way. The sad part about this setting is one may not understand that he or she is being driven by his or her complaints and not the desire to receive a true resolution to the problem. The information in this chapter will attempt to guide you down a narrow path of how truth, trust, and love work together as one in establishing a stronger character. Truth, what does this really mean and how is it applied is what people need to know. Truth is obviously derived from facts related to something that happened or something agreed upon (standards). When one looks at the basis of character then truth about the individual is derived from what one observes. The truths observed normally comes from what a person has been taught or picked up along the way in life. This is why it is important for parents to teach children moral value for this has an impact on the character one possesses. I always would tell my children be careful of the character traits you grab out the bag of traits for people will judge you when you express them, one way or another. Let's look at a person that has the trait of selfishness. Many believe that he or she can be selfish and keep people from noticing. What is not understood is when people notice something negative it is commonly taught to be polite and not throw a negative in someone's face which could lead to an argument. This teaching allows the selfish individual to believe he or she has mastered a form of manipulation only becoming bolder in the behavior. The problem is when confronted rather then be truthful about it anger or offense takes over. Now this happens in many phases of our interactions with people because it is hard to face the truth when the person is not ready to change his or her behavior. I say to people "***the hardest pill to swallow is the one not put together on an assembly line, the truth.***" This is because truth is the only medicine which cannot be broken down to fit an individual's consumption. Individuals do not pride themselves for being considered negative and this is true. I know, I know that many of you are thinking about now "I know someone who likes being negative" and I want you to know that is a front. Many celebrities and local people put on this front but at the end of the day all they want to do is be understood. Know this, if one should act out negatively this could be because this is what he or she has learned. Yet rest assured the day will come when the talk with that certain friend will reveal that he or she was just trying to get by, but that is not how he or she really is. Have you ever attempted to tell a friend or a lover about the things going wrong in the relationship and all is heard is his or her name connected to the incidents? The response is normally "so you are saying that I am doing everything wrong." You come back and say "then tell me what I have done to break us down" and they say "you expect me to remember everything right now at this moment?" HOLD ON, yes because it is at this moment the brain will send every memory pertaining to the conversation forward so it can be discussed. This is how the brain works, so if you cannot think of anything it is probably because the infractions were so minor that you never thought about breaking up over it. What is happening here is people do not like standing alone so the search for dirt to throw back is the next move. It is accepting the truth about one's self and the observation put forward which will forge the character to become what is necessary to positively bond the relationship.

Let's look at a positive character trait, responsibility. This trait will get relationships through hell and high water. Responsibility is a powerful process word and when applied properly soldiers will follow their leader to their own possible demise believing for the outcome of success. When a person is pointed out for doing good it is natural to seek to do better. When this person is pointed out for making an error or mistake, the intent to not repeat the situation becomes the priority by learning what is necessary. Responsibility brings about change so it is hard to go wrong here. The success of any relationship reaches full term when two people are responsible to one another. This commitment to being responsible to one another is what keeps the bond which no outsider can break. Another example here which can be used is infidelity (an affair) which is hard for many people to fully get beyond. Have you had the pleasure of knowing someone who is dealing with this issue and keeps bringing it up? The problem here could be the teaching or acceptance of how they came about accepting hurtful things which happen in life. There are many times a person sits in the circle of opinion conversation (back yard bar-b-que settings) and build their wealth of knowledge. Within the circle the old phrase "you can forgive but you can't forget" keeps coming up and people accept it to live by. The fight here is not forgetting it for once again the brain works with bringing memories to the forefront pertaining to the subject being discussed. I hope you caught the last sentence "pertaining to the subject being discussed" for the reason one cannot forget is because things have not changed causing the subject to surface again. The responsible thing to do is to discuss the surrounding facts that led to the affair and be *responsible* and commit to the solution. This may even mean quitting an event which will keep the significant other from trusting because this is where the affair was created. Remember the quality of a responsible person is to accept the error and then commit to the necessary changes for the situation to not repeat itself.

This is why an individual has to understand what it means to be truthful in every facet (area) of one's life for this will allow the understanding to why the necessary changes need to be made. This is why truth is so important because when two or more people are communicating there has to be a foundation of truth to refer to when things start going to left field. The quality of character here requires an honest look at one's self and then a measure of honesty to others to share what is true. When this step is neglected then the word truth becomes no more than a word and people cannot understand why chaos continues to rule. The sad thing is by the time one decides to tell the truth and accept responsibility all has been lost through the many battles.

The next topic is speaking on *trust* and how it piggybacks on truth. Many do not understand the functional meaning of trust and this is where many part ways. I want to share a thought about trust which many people do not often hear. I tell people there is a misconception about trust that is confused with respect. I recall throughout my lifetime people saying "one has to earn my trust" and this is totally not true. I know many of you are thinking I am wrong about this one. So, look how trust and respect are transferred between individuals and this will help one's understanding. I will start with respect for this needs to be cleared first to better understand trust. Respect is a form of courtesy given from one to another. On that note it is customary to believe if someone speaks politely to you then you return the favor and speak with politeness also. Now if someone yells at another then it is expected for the other person to yell back if the voices do not come down to talking level as a form of respect. This proves respect must be shown upon the first interaction or it may not be found in the return. It can only be said that *one must give respect in order to get respect.*

Now let us speak on trust. Trust only happens one way no matter how many arguments one will attempt to find to counter this point. Look at these points:

1. If an individual wants to borrow money and have been known for not paying back previously, yet they promise you they have changed.
2. If an individual who has not brought your car back on time and made you late for work, but needs to borrow it again.
3. If a former partner has lied and mistreated you and now want another chance because it will be different this time.

I could go on, but I believe I am making my point. The common answer to all of three scenarios pertaining to giving trust is the same. One has to loan the money before it can be paid back despite the previous disappointments. One must give the keys to the car before the person returns it. One must enter into the agreement to be in a relationship again before it can fail a second time. In conclusion trust must be given first and then and only then can one know if the person it was given to was worthy of the trust given. It is fair to say that trust is given and respect is earned.

If the characteristics which help to build this word do not exist within a person, then much will be lost. Trust is something someone has in a person based on the expectation that the person is genuine in character. Trust is something which is taught by example and then transferred to another so they may repeat the behavior. When raising children, the parent must be careful to not make promises they cannot keep. The constant letdowns will make the child believe he or she can trust nothing the parent says. There is a bigger problem at work here which many parents overlook. The transfer one may have taught the child is to be dishonest even though it was never directly taught. The child repeats the behavior of saying things they do not follow through with and when it is brought to them, they say "nobody's perfect." The point missed here is he or she is practicing the art of lying and playing it off like a scheduling conflict, just like the parent did.

If people cannot trust what one says, then what is the need of interacting with them. This might not seem like an issue to some, but look at how many people enter a vow of marriage and at first sight of trouble declare they should have never married. This behavior stems from not walking in the true character of trust, but lying to one's self to get what is desired *in the moment.* How many people sign up for cars or buy things from a rental store knowing they do not have the money for next months payment, but sign on the dotted line anyway. Now they spend the next few months dodging the collector and answering the phone with a foreign accent. This is one that really sets me back. How many people have an affair behind their mate's back lying about their whereabouts so they can spend time with the lover, only to now fool themselves in believing the lover will make a better partner? The problem here is the person cheating tells the lover how they made up some excuse to get out and on occasion has their friend cover them. Not many people look into the crystal ball to see this moment coming back full circle. When you foolishly fall in love with the one you are cheating with, he or she remembers all of those lies and connections therefore sending the relationship south from the start. Do you see there was nothing to trust from the beginning because the affair was formed from a lie because of the dishonesty behind the partner's back? This is why one will face a flurry of questions which will hinder the new relationship because of the trustworthiness which was never instilled.

People do not put a lot of value in the word trust, but wonder why their character is always questioned. Trust is one of the major cornerstones to the success story of any relationship and when not properly inserted into the equation then trouble looms. A major part of trusting someone is to see what you may not and keep your best interest at heart. This characteristic is important because when two people have a disagreement and a third party tries to chime in at the moment of distress, how should it be handled. This is where the partner expects the mate to always remember there is an active relationship and the trust of not breaking it is in play. This is why telephone numbers, emails, addresses, meeting places, photographs, and so on are deal breakers for trust. Why take them and then hide them from your partner only to explain they meant nothing. If the person you are with cannot trust you then who can they trust.

Love is the hardest of the three to control because many believe it is the one which controls you. Love can be the most precious emotion found to humankind, but it can also be the most dangerous. Love is a powerful emotion which can render a strong man weak and make a beautiful woman a slave to the one she gives her heart. Love hurts so bad because love requires one to give their deepest affections to obtain the pleasures it offers. This is why the characteristics of love can be overwhelming causing people to leave all behind to take up a life with someone they declare their love to. Love is made three times as strong when truth and trust accompany her side, but can become twice as dangerous when betrayed by the same two. People have learned to say the word love while losing the distinction between the meaning. Look at some of the things we love; our pet, our children, our mate, our jobs, our car, our food, our house, many more things. When a word is utilized so much one can lose the ability to properly use it in the appropriate manner. Examine this scenario, a couple has friends and they declare their love for one another. As life runs its course disagreements occur and the friends are called on more frequently to become a listening symbol of the couple's complaints. What many do not understand is a form of transference is happening. Love is a commitment between two people which goes well beyond any other relationship you will ever have. Love is to share one's complete self with the other in exchange for the same vow. The problem is that people believe the characteristic of love can be found in its genuine state many times over throughout life, unfortunately it cannot. Love in its purest form cannot be repeated for the things which breaks the heart always mend with scar tissue leaving it to never give the same again. If a person is repeatedly hurt through broken relationships then how much scar tissue covers the heart? Getting back to the couple who now is sharing their woes with each other's friends while unbeknownst to themselves they are destroying the relationships of all parties. The ability to honor each other has been destroyed when they share the other's downside while simultaneously creating division through judgement with the information given to the friends. Soon someone will notice the change in the way he or she is being treated and hell is the price to pay.

I often tell people that you will hate to the same measure in which you love and many do not believe it…at first. Life has a balance rather a person figures it out or not. There is good/bad, right/wrong, up/down, and many more, but for love there is hate. These are two of the strongest emotions known to mankind. Love will make you give all to a person and hate will spurn one enough to take the life of a person if taking their ability to finance a good lifestyle is not enough. This is why love is nothing to play with because the repercussion can be deadly. Look at the couples who declare they are in a love/hate relationship and are proud. The relationship is highlighted with insecurity, jealousness, envy, vindictiveness, destruction, and much more. Individuals will brag on how they keyed cars, shredded clothing, emptied the bank account, fought the cheating party of the mate, and so on. Yet after all of this the couple remains together believing the relationship can still work. Do you see now the grand delusion of love when trust and truth do not accompany her side?

One of the biggest mistakes made when it comes to love is having dyslexia in the field of love. One must understand that love is a process word as is the word falling. Imagine someone standing right in front of you saying they just stood up from falling, but you never saw the person fall. It would be impossible to believe it happened though they stand on it did. Imagine a person telling you that he or she loves you, but it seems like every interaction is a negative. This is because people do not understand these words are process words used with little to no understanding. To fall is to lose the ability to stand so the body crashes to the ground beyond one's control. If there is anyone around, they would normally run to your aid to see if everything is alright. Love is viewed by one's self and others because of the sweet things said and the considerable things done for one another. Then how do people come to the conclusion of *falling* in *love* at first sight? The answer is simple when honesty is used to find a conclusion.

A person normally has a preset idea of what type of person he or she is attracted to. The mixed signals happen when one stumbles across the person of desire and immediately closes the deal with saying those words, I have fallen in love. What one has found is a prototype of what he or she desires pertaining to the outer looks. One does not know enough about the individual to have been swept off your feet (fallen) and enough about the character of the person to make a good mate or the other parent of your children has not been concluded to consider love. This is what dating (process word) is meant to help one determine about the mystery man or woman. The problem is that if not careful one will use this time to get the three-week (or dates) rule out way to get to sex. If the sex is good then a couple has been formed while knowing very little about the other's life goals. This may help us to understand why the longer two people know each other the more divided they become (opposite of falling in love). Ask yourself this question "should you argue more in the beginning of the relationship, the middle, or as it is ending? I will give you a time frame to make the pondering easier, let's say ten years.

What is a solution to this issue?

The question here is "how does a couple capture all three in a relationship?" Well it is not easy, but it is able to be accomplished. When you meet someone fight the lustful instinct to see marriage based on his or her looks. This is the issue many people face because looks (facial or physical) is what is first seen. People need to be truthful with what it is he or she wants from the beginning for the long haul. This means, if a woman knows she wants to be married to a faithful man, have children, and do the death-do-you-part thing then start off on that note. It is not wrong to talk about your goals and desires from the beginning to learn if he is on the same path. Let me tell you talking about his favorite pizza, what movies he likes, his favorite actor/actress, and what he rates as a great kiss normally leads to heartbreak. It is simple, ask a man how many children he wants, does he want to own a home or remain living in an apartment, how often do you see your friends when you enter a relationship for life. These questions may lose the guy or girl early on, but it saved you a ton of headache in the end. Many say that sex clouds the emotions and this I personally believe is true. If one does not ask these questions and gets to the bed first and the sex is mind blowing, one will declare his or her love. What is funny with what happens next is now he or she will say as the relationship is falling, "he changed." No, he did not change, but you just never ventured down the right path to determine if he was the right man for your dreams and desires. Did you catch what I said there? I said the right man for your dreams and desires. Many get caught up on looks and stop there for looks makes other envy you, but character or should I say the lack there of, makes you envy him.

Asking certain questions will give you an insight to a person's character. Try asking a female what is her favorite meals to cook or the holiday she loves preparing for. If she says "I go to my mother's house" then there is reason to raise an eyebrow. This is not saying she does not cook, but I would ask another question to be more direct. What is your favorite meal to cook at home? The reason for this is because if you plan on making her a mate and then possibly a mother, then I would believe that you and the children would eventually get hungry and/or tired of fast-food.

Let me pick on the fellas for a minute to balance the score. If a man has a friend and he is attempting to make you his partner in life, but is always with his friend, then you may need investigate more. What you need to find out is how deep does this friendship run. A person should understand there are levels and phases everyone goes through in life, but there are only a few spots for priority within our lives. When people marry then the mate becomes the priority and as they have children the children become the second level of priority. This is where it gets tricky for the next priority is the commitment to the family financially. If anyone disagrees with this then that may explain why you have men or women not working to help keep the family priorities in check. One should not compromise the finances to go out with friends for this is how the arguments from the mate start pouring in. The priority stops at immediate family for the vow says *leaving mother and father and forsaking all others* and this is exactly what it means. I will speak more about this in a later chapter.

The point to this chapter is simple, be truthful with yourself from the beginning and then expect the same from the other person. Truth will build the trust needed to bond with their partner, and then love has no boundaries as all three work together to bring forth the happiness designed for life.

CHAPTER 4

Timing is everything

Character is something that has to be taught and then when the right time comes it shows itself to others. It is through the expression of character that relationships on every level is formed. Character is polished through moral values and as one interacts with people on a daily basis good or bad vibe grow from the interaction. From the time we are children the things we are taught are forming our character while shaping the friendships we will develop. It has been said "birds of a feather flock together" and this holds a bit of truth to it. People will gravitate to others like them for it makes interacting smoother. Many people call this fate and the misunderstanding is clear, but it will take a closer look at the subject to get a better understanding.

Many of the educated people will tell you that fate are events or circumstances which happen beyond a person's control. Before we go any further, I would like the record to show that I believe this also...to an extent. My problem is when is one is made to become accountable for his or her actions. This is why it is important to teach character so the generations will avoid the negatives in life and be around the positive people to avoid the negative outcomes. Look at the phases a child passes through to become an adult. I am going to speak in layman's terms for I do not want you to feel like you are in school. These are the phases:

1. Phase one: Infant to toddler is the time the parent is instilling naps, feeding, and nurturing for the baby's development. It is important to get the sleep patterns down especially if you have to return to work. The main concern in this phase is to monitor the development of the infant's health.

2. Phase two: Toddler to school age is the time to start focusing the child to use the mental development of the brain. This is when the teaching of the alphabet, how to do the basic counting, the identifying of colors, and word pronunciation should be taking place. This is also the first phase of their exploratory years (they will come again). School has exposed them to other characters.

3. Phase three: Pre-adolescent years would fall in line with the pre-teen years ranging from the age of about nine to thirteen. This is when a child would normally want to start leaving the yard to play and not be under the parent constantly because they have made a few friends. This stage is a warning to parents to be careful of the company your child keeps and know the teachings of the parents

for it will rub off on your child after so much time is spent in their company.

4. Phase four: Adolescent years normally range from fourteen to seventeen and will bring back around the exploratory years for this is the years the body develops and many children get that extra attention. These are also the years that the term boyfriend/girlfriend comes to surface with the hint of sexuality looming in the air.

5. Phase five: Adult
   Understand this, it starts from the time a child is taught to respect their adults at two years of age. When this is built on throughout the years, it is this teaching which dictates the major outcomes in a person's life.

Teachings when I was a child were taught to strengthen character like, respect your elders, if you do not have anything positive to say then say nothing, share with others and they will share with you, and so on. It is these teachings that help build the positive outcomes and avoid the people which can lead to the negative ones. If one will use the philosophy of this to understand the main relationship which means the most, then it yields a better understanding that it is not fate but one's decisions dictating the outcome. Let's bring this conversation into perspective of the book to gain a better insight. It is the teaching of respect for one's self and others from a young age that will hopefully help you be received by the teachers. The next phase the teaching does is hopefully help an individual to select the right people to become friends with. These first two phases are important for it makes life easier mentally when it pertains to having confidence on positive outcomes. The role the parents play within these years are important because it will showcase for the child what to expect in their upcoming roles when he or she enters relationships.

So many people want to shield our children from our disagreements rather than let the children understand the proper way to handle disagreements. Just because we disagree does not mean we have to become enemies. Let our children hear the disagreement as well as see the commitment to come to the table and figure out resolutions. One of the most important things to teach is composure, but the sad thing is that many do not even know what it is or when to use it. Composure is the ability to remain in control of one's self. This word alone should have made you think back on what I said earlier in this chapter about your decisions play a role in the outcomes you face. Teaching our children how to conduct themselves in every situation possible will help them to understand that timing is everything. A person does not have to agree with everything, but they will soon learn when timing is not right to express the difference. If a person is upset with their mate an hour before the families are coming over for Christmas, is it the right time to express it now as the families have arrived? Of course not, for you are out of line to your marriage and your children to cause such a disruption on this day. What example of composure do we give our children? If the timing is not right then it throws almost everything out of alignment.

I had a child who did not keep his or her grades up to par, but I would not belittle the child in front of the siblings as to not destroy the character being instilled. If I was to not show composure while dealing with the child at the moment of a parent's disappointment, then what have I done to build the child? Nothing, nothing at all. What I pass on to the next generation is that timing means very little when it comes to a person's dignity because of your disappointment. The disregard for timing at this moment destroys all of the good memories from the past and will hinder the building of memories from that moment forward. Timing is everything when it comes to the things we do or say.

Do parents give any thought to how it effects a child to be humiliated in front of his friends or classmates? Probably not! It is easy to get caught up in the misbehavior and allow the overload to make one believe to embarrass them in front of everyone will work. No, it does not for the mere reason that you have now made them the ridicule of their peers. This behavior is repeated throughout life and the mates and children of that child will probably be divided as they grow together. Let us talk timing when it comes to a child dating. I know this is a sticky subject, but it is one which needs to be tackled. I know many people will come to arms when it comes to the freedom of allowing children to date. Look at the key word in the last sentence for many of us hear it again as we evolve in our adult relationships, child(ren). If timing is everything then it really would apply here for dating and children is a bad combination. One must understand dating is a word which is openly accepted by the community. When a man or woman is spoken for then all other would-be pursuers should be put to rest. Look at the first contradiction so often overlooked, "man" or "woman." Then why are children openly dating with the parent(s) consent? What is amazing to me is when the parent finds out that the son's girlfriend may be pregnant the first thing said is "What were you thinking?" What should have been said is "How were you thinking?" This would open the door for the child to say to the parent that he or she was thinking like a child. See it is clear at that moment the parent realizes this child is not responsible enough to parent a child. Then why did you let them openly date? The answer is simple, the timing was not right for they are too young for this type of responsibility. I have a question on my mind in which I would like to share, if you do not mind, well of course you do not mind. How is it that fourteen is considered too young to date now, but from Adam to cowboy days fourteen was the prime age to start a family? The answer is simple once again for responsibility, morality, accountability, structure, and so on were taught then to prepare one for the family life to continue life on earth.

What appears to be happening is as the generations continued people fought for more freedoms. It is time to realize that we fought for so much freedom that we sacrifice many of the things which are meant to build strong character. Parents have to realize it is easy to become advocates for our children's demise. We do not want to say no to them for we do not want them angry with us. This is a part of the parenting process rather one is comfortable with it or not. When we turn the reins over to our children with little to no understanding then we have set them up for failure and it is simple as that. I know many of you are possibly wondering how did he raise his children, well I will tell you. I told my children from the start that it is my job as a parent to teach you how to handle life's issues, how to become a responsible individual, and to be a role model for you pertaining to the visual things you will learn from me. I continued by saying I did not mention boyfriend or girlfriend because you are not ready for that role until beyond my time with you. I know I cannot stop you from liking someone, but I am letting you know that a boyfriend or girlfriend will not be sitting in this house in that capacity. We will not be having the "he have been heartbroken" conversations. Lastly, I will not come to a school function and you will be sitting between some boy's legs or otherwise. Did I realize my children would do all of these things behind my back, well of course, so I had an alternate plan? I lectured my children on life every Thursday (amnesty night) this way they still received the information needed based on the life they are living. I informed my daughters of how boys will tell them what they want to hear to get where they are going. I told my oldest as she entered high school to watch how the upper-class boys will find her attractive and want to be her boyfriend. I asked her to trust what I am saying and at that moment ask him why is he picking me for you have been here for two to four years and watch him. It was about December of her freshman year when she came home and informed me that a boy in the twelfth grade approached her. She said that he wanted to know if she had a boyfriend and if not what about considering him. She asked him what I had said for her to ask and she said he just turned and walked away. The point here is, though I did not openly accept dating my children were still prepared for the obstacle's life will throw at them.

CHAPTER 5

We know what we want, but do we know what we need to be?

This chapter will focus on the individuals who want a partner of a certain character quality, but is not aware of the character in which he or she needs to be. People do not understand the problems they are creating is that their assessment is not complete when it comes to a relationship. One will evaluate what the other person's character is, but not look at does his or her character compliment the situation. How many times have you heard a friend say "I met someone who is everything I need?" This problem is what we will focus on for it is here the issues begin.

In my example I will use Benny and Tasha to show the point I am making. Benny was raised in a home which had a mother and a father in authority. There were six children all together and the family dynamics were average. The parents argued, but normally sought solutions, the children fought within the sibling rivalry. Though the bad existed there was the good things to help anchor the good characteristics for the children's future relationships. The father and mother worked, meals were cooked every day, accountability was instilled through chores and school as well as through role models. Tasha was raised in a home with four siblings and a mother which struggled because there was no father to assist with the children. Now the arguments were there (for this what children do), but regular meals and accountability lacked because the mother was working and attempting to live her life as well. Without the accountability school and chores do not become a priority in most of these cases so little is instilled.

The setting a child is raised in is important for it can raise his or her expectations or dim them. When an individual is raised in a negative situation, he or she can see the issues and set his or her sights to overcome them or just settle for the same thing. The latter only repeats the cycle and little has been learned, or one can break the cycle by acknowledging the problems with the way he or she was raised and then implement the solutions necessary. Understand a person will normally adapt to the environment in which he or she is common to. Few people (on a world scale) can come from under a negative setting and turn it around before they waste much of their life away.

Benny met Tasha at social function and was polite, cordial, and open. Tasha was impressed by his manners and the ability to talk on a broad scale. Tasha told her friends that she met the perfect man. Tasha never looked at her characteristics and how they will compliment a relationship with Benny. Let's look at Tasha's character coming out of her environment. Tasha learned how to survive, but in many of the wrong ways. When an individual is in a negative environment with little positives to lean on the strategy becomes "team me." People can become so negative that he or she cannot understand how the negativity lives on in the relationship. This happens because one will set up negative vices to replace the coping vices needed to keep the peace. Individuals will decide to avoid an argument by saying I just will not say anything so when the other person is talked out the session will end. This sounds like a plan for the moment, but it is disastrous in the end for no resolutions were found so the situation is bound to repeat itself. It is this repetition which will make the dream person eventually raise his or her voice and progress to name calling or worse. Now I am not saying this is right, but this is what happens.

What happens here is both people have expectations of how he or she wishes to be treated, but the problem is in the core of how he or she treats others. A positive person expects the other to render the same respects of listening, not rudely interrupting, speak to the context of the conversation to show understanding to the issue brought by the other, and to find resolutions to not repeat the situation by establishing boundaries of respect for one another. The negative person has expectations also, do not treat me like I treat you. It is clear this person is aware that his or her behavior is rude or out of line so he or she does not like it if it is done to them. These are the logs which fuel the fire because one has learned to talk it out and the other has learned to walk out.

Tasha will soon convince herself the relationship probably was a wash from the beginning and suggest a break. Benny may attempt to point out the problem and give the solutions to turn things around, but Tasha will only see that he will not let it go. This is clearly an example of what many couples do on a daily basis and cannot seem to get ahold of the problem. This is clearly the upbringing both individuals learned from. The problem many times with claiming to be a survivor is one can learn ways which are really considered selfish.

Look at a person who was controlled throughout his or her childhood and given little to say about their own life. He or she will promise to themselves that no-one will ever control me when I move out. The problem is the focus has become to over talk others, and possibly counter every decision given. The person sees this behavior as making his or her own choice, but not recognizing the character of fighting everything rather it be right or wrong, as long as I am not controlled.

It is this attitude which allows the person to see the peace the other person brings, yet not recognize the chaos he or she confronts it with. It is clear when individuals know what they want, but not many people look at themselves to see what they are to be in a relationship.

It was previously stated the environment a child is raised in can perpetuate this behavior, but let us take a look at what helps it to stick around. It is hard to know what one should become in a relationship without the proper knowledge. I mentioned earlier in the book about "birds of a feather flock together" and this is what I will speak on now.

This begins as a child for when children come together it is easy to complain about what they believe the parent(s) have done wrong. It is here the individual is learning how to establish negative associations which will guide their thought patterns ruining their future relationships. It is when one engages in negative conversation positive knowledge is not learned and this throws the balance of decision making off. A person can know that something is good for him or her, but will walk away from it in dispute because he or she have never mastered the art of finding resolution. Resolution is not found through complaining, but through reasoning and rationale.

If a female says that all men are dogs now that she has moved into her adult life, she loses the balance to her decision on men. It normally happens to be a group of women who share this opinion while forgetting they have not dated all men. In conversation people absorb what is said while losing the integrity of why it is said. She has only been open to the men (however many) in which she dated and clearly this does not cover all men. If she takes a closer look at herself to see what is it she may be overlooking with men (will not work, not a good reason for still living with mother, has no accountability towards household chores, likes to stay in the streets with his boys, and so on) then she may realize the problem. She may like men that present a lot of time for her, but lack quality character to build a positive relationship, this also goes for men.

Do you know someone that will call someone for advice and get the positive answer? It is because he or she may be negative so they will call ten other people to find the one answer which satisfies what they want to hear and settle on that. Try this on for size. Have you had a person expect someone not to get upset and call a name? This is what he or she expects of the other but cannot see what he or she is doing to lead to the issue of name calling. A person will cut you off when speaking and when asked not to a comment in the middle of a statement this comes forth "okay you can do all of the talking" when that is not the case. It is rude to interrupt someone when they are speaking and this is what he or she will tell you if you interrupt them. See how it is expected of one to do what is right while the other party does what they are common to doing.

It is easy to see in others what we expect of them so he or she can be happy, but many have to fight to get the same in return. I believe the issue here, if you listen to this you will see, is because a person is being judged and not accepted for who he or she is. I know this may be a bit to take in all at once, but allow me the opportunity to explain. When a person accepts you for who you are then he or she is proud of your accomplishments for they speak to the positiveness of the relationship. Example: When a woman is well spoken in the field of Arts and Craft and a question is raised to the husband on the subject. The husband has no problem handing it off to his wife for he accepts this is her field of expertise. Let us look at the flipside of this scenario. This is the position of the husband which judges his spouse springing forth envy when put in the same position. He says "ask my wife she seems to know something about everything." This comment appears to be harmless, but it is not for there is more under the surface than the natural eye can see.

The point here is when we come together it is good to know what we want in a person and how our life compliments his or hers. There should not be a problem because you have become one and the two goods of the couple will overshadow the small things that come up. If you have a partner who is punctual then be ready an hour early and stop expecting the partner to settle for being late. If you have a partner who is smart and knowledgeable then do not sit in ambush waiting on them to be wrong. These are the reasons you were attracted to them in the beginning. Grow the relationship and stop being the weed killing the garden.

CHAPTER 6

Where does your mate fall on your list of Accountability?

This chapter will focus on how does one list their mate in the chain of family and friends. This is possibly one of the biggest arguments which lead to breakups. When a partner does not have confidence in being the number one person there is a price to pay. It does relationships good to know the love which bonds us is spread equally across the character of the partner. Many of you are possibly wondering what that last sentence means. It simply means that it is fair to assume that people fall into a trifecta of expected character traits. The word is normally used in horse racing (to bet on three horses at one time), but I will use it for the purpose of defining a person.

Before we jump into that I want to give some background information which will help down the stretch. Our first encounter with prioritizing the list is our parents for they are who we meet first. The second people on the list is normally the siblings because you are born into the family. The third on the list would be the friends one makes along the way. The fourth on the list would be any associates through family, friends, and jobs. The last and final individual on the list is the partner one will meet.

If you are closely following along then you should see the pattern which is developing in front of you.

1. Parents
2. Siblings
3. Friends
4. Associates
5. Partner

The order is the reason I believe the confusion exist because you meet the partner last, but it is through the teaching one should be receiving that should clear the situation up. Look at the marriage vows for instance, they pertain to the last member on the list and then it should alter the list. The list should now look like this:

1. Husband/wife
2. Children
3. Parents
4. Siblings
5. Friends
6. Associates

The marriage vows clearly give instructions which say "leaving mother and father and forsaking all others" This is an indication to rearrange the list. Then why do we mess this simple instruction up? The answer is simple, because we are not taught it in its entirety. If you remember I pointed it out in the role definitions that the spouse is the only contract you sign bonding you to anyone on this earth.

Now the attention needs to focus on how did we get this far off center. This is another simple solution, but I will give you a few examples to illustrate.

Example 1. Babies are adorable and the parent falls in love with their new creation representing the two of them. Some parents (not all) fall so in love they forget the teachings of life for the child is to leave them not remain forever. There are situations in which a parent will make a child believe they are obligated to the parent until the parent's death. This is admirable for the child to take care of the parent if it should come to that, but by no means is it an obligation. The parent should have taken care of themselves throughout life so as they age it does not become a burden on the children or other family members. This teaching can be one reason why many children keep the parents at the top of the list. Why do you think some relationships are hindered by females that are best friends with their mother or men acting as momma's boys? Now come on and do not back out on me now for you know you have heard of these situations. The problem is one will make the spouse think that he or she is second to the parent. Many of you know that you may be living this situation right now as you are reading this chapter. Don't run out, but talk about it and attempt to hopefully shift the list into the correct order.

Example 2. A woman's bond to her child is believed by many to be precious and I agree. Yet one must still remember the child(ren) never comes before the spouse for the two of you are bonded and the marriage vow pertaining to this is "forsaking all others" that's right, I said it and it does not change what it means. Children are a procreation (reproduction, offspring) to fill the numbers on the earth, but the spouse is until death do you part. Children graduate and leave to start their own lives around 18-20 years of age. Well unless your reading this with your 40-year-old live in son sitting next to you, just teasing. Like it or not that beautiful being the two of you brought into the world falls under "forsaking all others" do not blame me I did not write it. Together you stand in authority over the children teaching them so they may one day face the world without you constantly by their side, for that is the role their spouse will take over. Did you catch the shift in the list within that last sentence, if not, read it again until you get it?

Example 3. A child spends much of their early years bonding through agreements and disagreements with their siblings. There are times when the relationship is so good people make sidebar bonds for life. I will agree it is good to have a close-knit family and it is great that siblings get along as children, but it does not take away the need to shuffle the list. I can hear somebody thinking what about twins, triplets, and so on. They still fall under the list as siblings so the shift should be expected, like it or not. It is these bonds or deals in which one makes as a child (without proper understanding) and then attempt to uphold as an adult bringing about their own demise.

Example 4. As a person develops friendships, they share secrets they otherwise would not share with a family member because the friend does not live in the home so the secret appears more secure. There becomes some form of an allegiance and they become thick as thieves. Have you watched those entertainment shows where the guest says "this person has been my friend through my last five partners," well do you wonder why? It is because he or she does not understand the list needs to be shifted. People think the allegiance is valued based on the timeframe (timeshare) of knowing the friend versus the partner, wrong. The value to the friend (based on time) is superseded by the love for the partner, so the shift should be adjusted. I will let this also stand for associates (which was the next step in the list) to kill the repetition. You cannot timeshare

Example 5. The partner is the bell of the ball, the cheese on the macaroni, the cream of the crop. I love this one for it is the most honored of all. As you know from the first list the partner is the last one the person meets. How can you tell if you are still working on the first list when it comes to your partner? This is seen if you ever find yourself saying to your partner during a disagreement these words "a reliable source told me something about you." Who should be more reliable than your partner? This is why the value of relationships cannot stand on who was known the longest because the partner would not stand a chance. Many do not understand the value of all relationships is built within the heart. The first list shows the partner is the last person one will meet, but the second list shows after one gives their heart to another the portion given is larger than all of the others combined. If your mate does not own 51% of your heart then you may need to reevaluate your relationship list.

I spoke about the trifecta earlier and I base it on the make-up of a human being. I believe an individual has three phases of personality (character) which makes up the one person others meet. I will attempt to convey to the reader this view through a series of illustrations to help you understand my position.

When two people meet it is obvious the visual of a person is what one will see and many times already decide this is the one for me. It is here the mistake is made which will come back on us in a negative way. There is so much that is missed with this quick irrational judgment leading to the arguments and possible breakup which lies ahead. As I recently stated pertaining to a person being threefold in character, explained by the word trifecta.

This is the layout in which I refer to leading to people never adventuring to find this in a person because we tend to stop at looks. Every man or woman has three phases of character as an adult which must be active for a relationship to hit its full stride. When one should examine the words "man" or "woman" one must understand this is merely the shell which houses the three main characteristics of the individual necessary for a successful relationship. Here is how the breakdown looks:

Man   *Woman*
Male---takes care of oneself---Female
Mate---takes care of a mate---Mate
Father---takes care children---Mother

This is the trifecta in which I refer for this best describes what a person should bring to the table to make a relationship successful. To clear my path for you race horse fans I will explain it so that you can follow along. I am aware the word is used in racing to mean if one bets on at least three horses to place in a racing event. A straight bet is to say these certain horses will place in this order. A box bet is to simply say these three horses will come in the top three spots. Now that I got that out of the way let us continue. The chart above is showing the different levels of responsibility every person must meet to have a true impact in the relationship.

When you come across people during the day it is how they dress which catches our attention. If they are dressed nice (depending on what you like) then it is accepted they are responsible for themselves (phase one). Now the question becomes, how would you know if he or she is ready for phase two until you jump in. The answer once again is simple. From the time you exchange numbers with a person does not mean that you are now dating as in a couple. This time slot in between (exchanging numbers and deciding to call this a relationship) is meant to gather information about the person. If one should truly listen to a person then he or she will give indications of their future plans. What you hear will give insight on rather phase two and three is in their sights. Look at this: if a male and female go out on their first date (this does not mean a couple has formed) the purpose is to talk so each one can gather information to determine if this person is worthy of becoming a life partner. The first problem I see here is most people think the word "date" means a couple has been formed therefore we are dating. Well, what about when businesses have lunch or dinner dates with clients? What about when two friends who have not seen each other in years set a lunch date? Can you see now where the confusion is? If the person meets phase one then the plans to eat together has already been determined as a couple has been formed.

If the proper steps are taken then as the two engage in conversation normally people share what are their future plans. This is the time to listen for what happened in prior relationships to give you an idea was he or she the problem (phase two qualities). This is the time to listen to find out if children are in their life or if they are interested in children (phase three qualities). Watch how the conversation is driven from here. The answer about the past relationships will open the door to things one can identify about the person across the table. This information is an insight to who you are compared to the things highlighted (good or bad) about the prior partners. This will definitely give you an upfront perspective about a relationship with this person if you get past the looks and be honest with yourself. Understand if the person tells you something not liked by the prior partner and you know you do those things, then walk away or expect to change. If the opposite happens and you fit the bill on the things they expect in a partner, then a relationship may be worth the adventure. I know many people hate to be compared to a person's ex, but the conversation is necessary. See, if you hear things about the ex and compare yourself to the good and the bad, make the necessary changes so the relationship does not come across the same problems, then that person would never have to compare you for you already did it and made the changes. The conversation can build around the answer of if children are present. This can lead to if they want children (why or why not), or if they have children how often do they visit (noncustodial parent), or what activities they do with them (custodial and noncustodial parent). The trifecta of the person is like the horse betting, for you win if they have acquired the three phases (no matter the order) in real time or a processed thought.

This information about the person only strengthens the reason to prioritize the list. When you know you have found something more precious than gold, then you value it and will do as little as possible to lose it. One is accountable several times over in life to others (teachers, work, parents, children, and other events), you are accountable to your partner until death do you part.

I want to share this point of misunderstanding which is important. A person who informed another of the reasons for the prior breakups is not comparing the other to the ex. The person is sharing the disappointment of how upon knowing the history with the ex, the person knowingly lied while realizing he or she is of the same persuasion. The disappointed individual should not have been put in the situation to compare if the other party had been honest from the beginning instead of selfish.

This chapter may have brought forth some debate, but hopefully good debate. If one will give true thought to the things put forth it will strengthen your knowledge about your partner and make for a better life.

CHAPTER 7

Should people be opened minded to all things?

This is another subject in which I enjoy having with people for I am always amazed with people sharing the dandiest beliefs. This topic has been an age-old argument for many people. Understanding what it means to have an open mind is what will keep unnecessary stressors away. Many individuals harbor the fear that being open minded is to be easily swayed or tricked by others. This is far from true, for to have an open mind allows one to see and hear so much more.

People do not understand as you meet others there are going to be things that differ from what you are used to doing. This by no means makes them wrong, but an open mind will allow you to categorize how you fit the individual into your life. There are different personality traits which allow people to closely associate or maintain a distance between each other. Now when we are speaking about relationships the same rule applies. One has to first think it is easy to justify what you do for you have lived with yourself all of your life. What is not fully understood is as you close your mind to things which are not familiar to you then you are blocking others out. Remember we all come from differently taught backgrounds though they may be similar in ways. I will give quite a few illustrations as to relate to the many issues different readers may experience.

An open mind is important to have as people come and go throughout your lifetime. Interactions become unbearable if you close your mind to understanding why people do the things they do. A common mistake is that people think it is okay to not listen to things if they do not do them that way. This is wrong in every sense. You can hear much more than people are telling you when your mind is open to various views of the subject. To understand why your partner has no problem with bathing on a regular basis, or farting and believing it is funny…at the dinner table is frustrating. The biggest thing that you are faced with at the moment is the person is already your partner and you cannot figure out how did you miss this behavior.

The missed behavior is easy to explain for it is because people put on their best behavior for you in the beginning. Well how does having an open mind play into this? One has to understand people have different ideas of what is funny and what did their parents enforce in the field of hygiene's.

Example 1. It is easy to laugh at a child when they fart, but remember the teaching to respect others is still necessary and the laughing should fade in time. If the teaching is not instilled the child goes through life farting and overlooking the disgust on the faces of others. The problem is at the moment you are smelling the fart which is destroying your appetite, you really can give a darn about what his parents laughed at. This can be another issue when someone farts under the covers on a nightly basis. Again, at the moment one does not give a darn about laughing because you want to go to sleep, but they think its's hilarious. This is where the open mind kicks in so you do not destroy the life you have together over something you are just realizing.

Example 2. What about the lack of attention to body maintenance? It requires an open mind as well for you have to understand the dating process allowed prior warnings to when you were coming over, so a shower was taken. Now that you live together the prior warnings have been taken away and now one realizes this person may be nasty. I am laughing right now so give me a chance to regain my composure…okay I am ready. What about stinky feet? Once again, the ability to buy new socks or gym shoes have been taken from the person to prevent you from knowing. One is probably wondering "how does an open mind pertain to this issue?" Well, it is because the person is now your partner and you have to figure out a way to communicate to them as well as understand the person you are now meeting.

Example 3. This one is for the men who may be reading this book. Yes, men have to have an open mind as well. This is a big one for this is heard in comedy, radio shows, and your inner circles, but I am going to say it anyway. Men will complain about the woman becoming a witch at those certain times of the month, better known as her menstrual cycle (period). The sad part about what I am getting ready to explain many women which I spoke with could not explain this to me, and they have the menstrual cycle. Let me set the mind first by hopefully pulling some memories which will aid me in conveying this point. Do you remember the scene in movies when someone got shot but they give a speech before they are to die? They say something like "I just need to rest and I will be okay" and then their head falls to the left or right and they die. Do you remember when your father or mother did not get enough sleep over the course of a week or so and they became grouchy? Did you have a father who worked a hard labor (physical) job and upon returning home the word was "do not bother your father for he has had a hard day." Why are people told to rest for a few hours after donating blood or having extensive bloodwork performed? What is similar about all of these situations? You guessed it *fatigue!* What! Well of course it is.

The blood carries oxygen throughout the body so when you lose blood the body experiences fatigue and consistent fatigue is expressed through angry or frustrated channels. This is where it pays off in having two people switching off on the family responsibilities, especially when that time of the month comes around. I cooked, cleaned, washed-dried-and ironed, and kept up with the children, as the children's mother can attest to this. I never have had those "time of the month" arguments because she was able to rest. This is why having a man who can help around the home is important to the woman. So, men let's step up and women make smarter decisions. Men must understand the woman has been losing blood all day and the frustration mounts and then is expressed when faced with all of the home responsibilities. Men we cannot do anything concerning the hormonal changes the woman goes through, but we can do more within the home.

Example 4. One of the largest percentages people are not open minded to is insecurity. Many individuals look for the perfect mate only to become insecure. I have spoken to many people who think insecurity is a bad word and do not want to admit it. It is not, but it is an eye opener to undue stress if one will just admit it.

Look at it this way to help you bring it into perspective

with your relationship. A person has a car that is known as a beater, hooptie, junker, jalopy, and known by other names. The person has little problem worrying about noises outside which could pertain to the car because of its condition. The person is constantly on the look for a new car to dump the old one. When a new car is purchased a sense of insecurity can set in because the worry of the value and loss can be overwhelming.

The point being made here is one may not realize the inner insecurity which lies dormant inside until you get that one person which can unleash it. Simply put, there is no reason to be insecure when you really do not like the person you feel stuck with. This may keep you from understanding yourself completely until you find that person that you do not want to lose. It is now one can rise to the level of war when you fear the opposite sex speaking to the partner. It is now you may question their whereabouts for the fear of infidelity. It is now when they put on dress clothes you may question where they are going.

There are times an open mind to how different events entering our lives is needed to really know who we are and what we are capable of.

Example 5. This one is huge for it is the lack of an open mind when it pertains to communication. Now this may be a long section because there is so much which goes into this discussion. If a person is not open minded to the proper way to communicate then a long road lies ahead. I will try to be as precise as I can here for many relationships fall over this issue only to realize ten years down the road there was hope.

I constantly tell people the court room is the epitome of how a conversation should look, but the two of you play all of the roles. On that note let us look at the roles:

1. Judge: the main reasoner in the room
2. Jury: selected to weigh the facts
3. Prosecutor: to prove the charge
4. Defense: to prove the innocence
5. Accused:
6. Accuser:

Now that we know the roles one must understand how the roles pertain to the couple. The courtroom platform is one big conversation played out using multiple people to help in determining the truth. Before I can move on, I feel the need to clear an important word used in these types of conversations that has been taken out of context. The word is *argument* for many have become so used to the yelling and calling names while discussing issues the true meaning has shifted. When a court proceeding opens the judge says "counselors, present your opening arguments." By no means does this mean to emulate what people have reduced this to mean at home. So, now let's get back to how to communicate.

If there is an argument between individuals then the individuals become all of those positions. There is one more thing to add to the equation and that is the parties need to agree to be honest with each other on the points made. A stigma which hinders this process in which I am about to share with you is one's lack of ability to see what the other is saying from his or her position. For instance, if the conversation is about one of the parties is attempting to convey to the other that always being away from home is breaking the trust. The party which is doing all of the running cannot say "I do not see a problem" for it is not you sitting at home forced to wonder. There are times when you have to place yourself in the other persons shoes to gain a better understanding.

Now that we have covered all of that lets discuss the roles and their importance. In a courtroom the judge is the one to allow the conversation to stay on course of the subject which brought everyone there. If a lawyer is saying something during cross examination and the other attorney believes it is not proper then an objection is made. The judge will hear the reason for the objection and render a quick decision to uphold or deny the objection. The jury is to render a decision after carefully listening to both sides of the story. The attorneys are there to point out the facts to prove their story is the correct one. The accused and the accuser are to tell the truth from the best recollection of their memory. This is how it is supposed to go when the truth is really being sought.

Let's look at a conversation between two people in a relationship when one does not display an open mind. The setting is a discussion between Benny and Tasha (remember them) is taking place from an argument which took place a week ago. The argument centers around Tasha's oldest child (who is not Benny's child) always misbehaving, here we go.

Benny: Can we talk about the other day.

Tasha: I don't see the reason for you made it clear that Sonya is not your child.

Benny: No, I said you make me feel {Tasha interrupts}

Tasha: It doesn't make a difference because if a man is going to be with me, then he must accept my child.

Benny: You are going down the wrong path for I said you treat me like I am not her father even though I discipline all of the children the same.

Tasha: That's not how I heard it or took it.

Benny: Do you deny this is what I said?

Tasha: I really don't care so move on to the next issue.

Benny: Well, this for instance when you cut me off because you don't want to hear it and {Tasha interrupts}

Tasha: Because you don't be talking about anything important. You be just complaining about *My Daughter Sonya*.

Benny: There you go with identifying her as your child, but I took her on when I married you.

Tasha: You didn't do anything special for that is what a man should do, huh.

Benny: You see how you speak in circles.

Tasha: You right there with me. It takes two, baby boy. {End scene}

This conversation would be a stressor for sure for it will never end. There is clearly not an open mind. Looking at the roles: **Judge:** Tasha and Benny

Attorneys: Tasha and Benny
Jury: Tasha and Benny
Accused: Benny
Accuser: Tasha

In a setting like this both parties have to work equally to keep the conversation on course. Both parties have to be willing to hear the others objections with an open mind while establishing the truth. Both parties must weigh the feelings the other expresses. If the accused has proven the feelings against them are ill-gotten then the accuser must readjust the feelings which have been establish. Many couples face this problem and do not have an idea of how to turn it around.

Example 6. This last example is an eye opener when this is thrown in your face. How can one be open minded when someone says "I was like this when you met me?" It is hard to be open minded, but it is still expected under these circumstances. I know this is not what a person wants to hear at his particular moment, so this is why I want to take you back to point of meeting each other. When two people meet is where the things accepted about one another at that time is what will be argued about later. If an individual is not working and shows no desire to look for a job, then it is fair to say that it is accepted money will always be an issue. It is fair to say if a person says that cooking is not a priority for other family and friends cook for him or her. Then when the person who was told this is hungry, anger should not be expected for you were aware.

In these scenarios pointed out it is easy to argue and possibly separate. What couples must find the ability to do is to be open minded. This is important for it will help in resolving what are the correct steps to take moving forward.

CHAPTER 8

Flirtation, cheating, and how we hinder our own relationship?

This chapter is really going to touch the people with too much of an open mind. There are boundaries a relationship must have in order to keep the love intact for one another. As society has evolved from generation to generation the meanings of many of the words used have evolved also. People tend to change the meaning of the words based on their complaints or desires for something different. The focus for this chapter will center on intimacy and flirtation and how it branches out to other forms of attraction.

The problem which has been encountered between couples is when intimacy comes in the form of flirtation and is spread to those it shouldn't be. The evolution of this form of flirtation has been perceived as making the love bond stronger. Not many cases have come to the full fruition of happiness based on this belief, yet many keep trying it anyway. I have listened to married couples argue because of the despair they live in and they have tried everything. Many have tried going to strip clubs together, threesomes, allowing the mate to have an affair, or some other forms of keeping the fire going. Many will delusion themselves into believing these forms work, but they do not for listen to their complaints to family and friends. It does not work because intimacy is a bonding tool and flirtation is a tool of destruction when shared outside a relationship.

I was once acquainted with a female who said to me that she likes a jealous man. I told her that I am not the one for her and she asked why not. I explained to her that jealousy leads to a mindset of insecurity and that leads to not believing your mate. I continued by saying it can only go downhill from there. She asked me how for she believes it could spark a deeper desire for one another. I sternly disagreed by saying it will most likely lead to arguing and then, at worst, fighting. She disagreed (and she has that right), but the last I heard about her marriage is that it was volatile and she divorced after nine years.

Many do not understand that intimacy is better connected to love and flirtation is more acquainted to lust. I will go as far to say these two are mortal enemies within the walls of a relationship when the latter is shared with others. The two traits, in which I speak, are pulling in two different directions and this is why a relationship can fail. This is why if a person wishes to live a life of flirtation then it may be best suited to remain single in status. When a person shares their intimate side with another it bonds them building the love they share.

If one should look at the impact flirtation has on a relationship (when shared with others) then it may become clearer. Flirtation evolves from the desires of a sexual attraction towards one another. This cannot be tolerated when two people are in a relationship because all of your sexual feelings should be toward your partner. I know many of you believe that outside flirtation will not hinder what you have with your partners and believe I am typing in error. Well I am not, so we will continue. The problem is many people are stuck in the mentality that flirtation is the best time of a relationship. NEWS FLASH, the reason flirtation is so high is because you have not moved into the relationship phase yet. Please think about this for a minute, for this is why sexual interaction is so high in the beginning. Once the moment has moved on two people normally find themselves getting through the day, without sex.

Flirtation occurs when you are looking through the eyes of lust to fulfill visual desires. Imagine when some people steal from department stores and how it all came about. A desire to have something which is not theirs builds through window shopping. Window shopping is to keep looking at things one cannot afford, but wanting the item grows all the more. If one is caught up in the moment, he or she will devise a plan to acquire it when no-one is looking. Flirtation works the same way and this is why it destroys a relationship when it is shared with others. I will stop there and come back to this point.

Now let us talk about intimacy. Intimacy is more respectful and inviting than straight lust. The root of intimacy derives from a companionship which is stronger than any friendship. This is a bond between two people that no outsider should be able to break. I often share with people: *"no-one can break two people apart unless one of them already decided to no longer be there."* True intimacy will cut off the need to want to be flirtatious with outsiders for one should have everything needed inside the relationship.

Remember earlier I spoke about window shopping and flirtation destroying relationships. It is flirtation (lust factors) one will lean on when first meeting someone. Please do not think a form of flirtation cannot exist for your mate, but the majority of your feelings will come through intimacy. This intimacy will fight the need of one's partner flirting with an outsider. The lack of intimacy will explain why many people get on entertainment shows and admit the new found desires for the third party. This could be because one is slow at building intimacy through respect for the partner. This keeps lustful eyes in the streets monitoring potential lovers.

Flirtation is good for the 100-meter dash and then it will run out of gas. This is about the time, if you continue and honestly bond with the other person, intimacy will take over. Intimacy will give the couple the ability to run the marathon of life and never give up. This is why the mentality cannot be comprised of accepting that an outside person is going to make the relationship better. How many people watch porn, but still believe the person is not turned on by him or her? How many people attempt to deal with the window shopping (calling it boy or girl talk) only to realize the partner cannot be trusted? This happens because outside flirting takes away from the relationship bonding. It does nothing but build on negativity between the two and the doom and gloom of the relationship begins.

When two people connect through intimacy then the trust between them is boundless. I have had the pleasure of going out of town for weeks at a time and I played the Xbox in my hotel room. I had no reason to go out because my partner was not there and understand that I represent both of us even in her absence. I have no reason to believe she does not feel the same. It is the respect for one another and the things accomplished which motivates intimacy upon the return to each other's presence. A rule of thumb to protect me at work was to never talk about my family affairs. I am not speaking on children in sports, but definitely I did not field questions about my partner. Some people will prey on this conversation to find vulnerable spots in your relationship.

One will be surprised how quickly flirtation can happen and trick you up. I have asked people do they really understand how cheating works pertaining to a relationship. Many do not know and this is why they live in their own demise. Anything one gives to an outsider normally is taken from the partner. This is a form of cheating. If a person does not talk with their mate, but finds the ability to speak to someone else about the ill-gotten feelings, that's cheating. The partner has to have the right to know what he or she is doing wrong so a chance to address will allow a change. If a person spends more time with their friends than their mate, the mate is being cheated bonding time.

There is a form of cheating which can lead to outside flirtation. There are people out there who are attracted to you and you may not be aware. Do not get me wrong here for I did not say the person wants to marry you, but they just bed who they can. They pick at you about the stability of your relationship and it sounds like casual conversation. If you start fielding questions about your relationship they are listening to see if it is sound or can they slip in. How many people complained to their "best friend" about their partner only to find out the friend is sleeping with the partner. Do I have your attention now?

Many times, we are playing the match maker between our partner and others. I can hear many of you asking, how? The answer is simple. It is not good to take your single friend out to dinner with you and your mate. Do you not realize you are allowing them to conversate finding a connection? It is not good to take your friend to a dress up setting or to the beach, for your mate is not blind. This is a few things couples think nothing of when inviting the single friend to tag along. So, think about how the two of you met and what bonded you. This is exactly how many affairs begin (not all) in these situations.

I am by no means saying a couple cannot have friends who are single, but be careful of the time spent. He or she is your friend so if one plans to do couple things then have them bring their partner. I hope many of you do not confuse this advise with being insecure. Insecurity is when nothing is there, but much is made of it. This advice is to open one's eyes to the fact of the friend and the partner are becoming playful and it is brushed off as friendly banter. This banter is what gets under the radar and then an affair occurs. One must always be mindful to the issues which can create breaks between two people, even when it is by one's own hand. It is hard to see at times because one is just happy the friends and partner are getting along.

People must understand when you have your friends spend the night and he or she wears nighttime attire, imaginations go to work. Some people miss this because deep down inside the friends is their way to not be alone with the partner they no longer can tolerate. This is still not a good move.

CHAPTER 9

Relationship repair, despite the damage

This chapter will focus on the relationship which has experienced some bad weather. This will also look at the ability to repair the damage no matter how bad. We will take a look at what kind of person does it take to turn a bad situation around by identifying what kind of worker you are, "construction" or "demolition?" I will attempt to give different scenarios as to connect with as many readers daily struggles.

Problems in a relationship tend to develop from our childhood behavior. Now I am not diving into every behavior, but I want to speak on manipulation and honesty. This is important because these two are silent and normally pointed traits out when something happens good or bad in an outstanding way. It appears that many of the characteristics of a person evolve around these two. As we maneuver through this narrow passage let us stay together so in the end, we at the least, gain an understanding.

It is as a child one learns the art of manipulation or the art of honesty. The chosen art will play a role in the character and personality one will develop.

When children take the path of manipulation it appears to be rewarding because of the material things coming their way.

Many do not understand that no characteristic stands alone so the manipulator has learned how to lie, to act in false pretense, and may have to become a demeaning person to sell the act. You know how a child will pretend to cry to get the parent to back off, it is still there as an adult. The reward is he or she diverted the deserved discipline. It may appear to be a way of life which is satisfactory for now, but in the end, no-one will fully respect you.

When a child takes the path of honesty there will be times when he or she will miss out on things because of telling the truth. The reward comes later, but the road is not as rough. If a child does something worthy of discipline and the punishment is canceling a plan because he or she owned it, then so be it. If all goes as planned then the child realizes to do what you are told is to go places you ask, problem solved. The child then earns the respect of others along the way.

Let us now look at how these two traits play out in relationships in the adult world. I will begin with the problems the manipulator faces giving a few insights to where things go wrong. I will remind you of a few key traits the manipulator must learn to display in mastering the art:

1. Lying
2. Acting
3. Demeaning
4. Escape

A manipulator has to control the context of what is going on to perform his or her best work. This explains the need to know all parties involved so the scripts can be revised like a director directs. A manipulator does not consider the work performed as outright lying for only a few minor details have been altered to gain the desired outcome. If there becomes any question to what has been said then the manipulator kicks into those self-taught acting lessons. This is a huge, do not ever believe the manipulator is an arguer for you are wrong. The manipulator is looking for a way out to escape the truth coming to light. Be clear, for the argument that you believe you are hearing is no more than a front to make you doubt yourself and let the subject go. When all else fails because you are holding to what you believe (but most likely cannot prove) the name calling or threats to end the relationship is put on the table. This is to make you believe that he or she is willing to throw in the towel on the relationship so you will let it go to keep them. In this role play the setting is Robbie is an ex high school athlete who has not given up his flirtatious ways. Carol is his wife of four years and they have two children.

Carol: Robbie can we talk.
Robbie: I hope this is not another one of your accusations.
Carol: {chuckles} I hear you, but seriously I want to talk about when we were out the other night at the club.
Robbie: What about it? I hope your insecurity isn't kicking in again because you know how this went the last time.
Carol: Well, I hope not for I am asking pertaining to what I saw.
Robbie: What did you see?
Carol: As I was returning to the table from using the women's bathroom, I noticed you leaning in close speaking in a woman's ear. She was smiling and then it looked as if she punched your number into her phone. I wanted to come to you rather than sit on it.
Robbie: First of all, you cannot believe everything you see for it can fool you based on your own insecurities.
Carol: I know and this is why I am coming to you.

Robbie: It was loud in the club so people have to get close to hear each other and I cannot account for her smiling that must be my charm and charisma.

Carol: What about the phone texting?

Robbie: I don't know what you are talking about there.

Carol: You have been getting text messages all of a sudden and when I am around you it appears that you give quick responses.

Robbie: Girl, that is your imagination for this is the typical signs of someone insecure being paranoid.

Carol: Then show me your phone so I can know that it is my insecurity.

Robbie now demonstrates the acting and demeaning behavior to find an escape.

Robbie: This what I am talking about, you go off on these silly accusations because I spoke to a woman and she laughed. You don't see how lucky you are that I chose you, but I am done with this for you will not stop.

Carol: No, just forget that I said anything because I may be wrong and jumping to conclusions again. I am sorry and I wasn't trying to accuse you.

Robbie: That's fine, I am going to run to the mall and will be back in an hour or so, love you.

Carol: Love you too! {End scene}

Take note on how he had an idea of what was on her mind from the beginning. The manipulator did not completely lie for he never denied leaning in to speak or the woman laughing. He throws it back to her insecurity (hinting at previous arguments along these lines) and says the laughing is because of his charm. When pushed for the phone number he never says no, but the acting kicks in. He throws prior allegations out there to slow down her assault to finding the truth. He reminds her of how lucky she is to have him and shows his willingness to end it all right now. She buys it and backs off. He then goes about his day as usual, he escaped.

This happens more than one realizes, but it plays out so fast one does not realize that he or she has been taken on a ride.

The other trait is that of an honest person and I will list the traits which walk along with being honest.

1. Trusting
2. Respected
3. Peacefulness

Now let us take a look at the same scenario from an honest take.

Carol: Robbie can we talk.

Robbie: Sure, what's on your mind?

Carol: I want to talk about when we were out the other night at the club.

Robbie: What about it?

Carol: Well, I want to share with you something I saw you do, but I want to give you a chance to explain.

Robbie: What did you see?

Carol: As I was returning to the table from using the women's bathroom, I noticed you leaning in close speaking in a woman's ear. She was smiling and then it looked as if she punched your number into her phone. I wanted to come to you rather than sit on it.

Robbie: First of all, I realize my past actions can make you insecure so I am good with this conversation.

Carol: I am glad and this is why I am coming to you.

Robbie: It was loud in the club so people have to get close to hear each other and I cannot account for her smiling that must be my charm and charisma. She did ask for my number and pulled out her phone, but I didn't give it to her.

Carol: What about the phone texting?

Robbie: I don't know what you are talking about there.

Carol: You have been getting text messages all of a sudden and when I am around you it appears that you give quick responses.

Robbie: Girl, that is your imagination for this is the typical signs of someone who has been betrayed, but that was my boys teasing me.

Carol: Then show me your phone so I can know that it is my insecurity.

Robbie now demonstrates honesty

Robbie: Here, take a look at the one- and two-word responses.

Carol: No, just forget that I said anything because I may be wrong and jumping to conclusions again. I am sorry and I wasn't trying to accuse you.

Robbie: That's fine, I am going to run to the mall and will be back in an hour or so, love you.

Carol: Love you too! {End scene}

Notice how Robbie was honest from the beginning causing Carol to trust his openness. Robbie was willing to understand how his prior decision making made Carol question his actions and maintained Carol's respect. In the end it is the first two traits which allowed the peace of the home and relationship to not be interrupted with unnecessary stress.

In relationships the problems which exist normally stem from dishonesty by one if not both parties from the beginning. One may not realize the conversations shared between the two of you should be met with honest answers or it should not be brought to the table. Lying upfront never turns out for the good because time and circumstances always catch up to you. Think about when you tell a person that you only a few relationships under your belt and you know it is a lie. Now as you are attending family functions one of your family members are not aware of the lies you told and speaks the truth. The family member is so-called complimenting you on settling down and says to the partner "Thank goodness for you because this was a wild one here, no-one ever thought he or she would marry." Can you imagine the conversation on the ride home and then on into the night about what you told them which made them choose you?

Now I have had people argue, but that is my past and it is really not their business. I can agree to a certain extent and this is why. If you had not answered the question in the beginning and established that point, I agree. Where people go wrong is, they begin having conversations on things about their past which really are irrelevant to this new relationship. Now I understand that a person wants to clear any criminal issues for this would be fair. What one has to understand is you do not need to ask questions to find out if a person is hyped on sex to establish if he or she is a dog. Simply stay out of the bed and watch and listen. If a person is constantly trying to get to the bedroom then it is clear of their intentions.

What he or she is doing with you is the pattern of what he or she has been doing before meeting you. A relationship can make it despite the failures, but one must look at the character of a person to help determine what problems one may face. Someone is thinking now "you can't know everything," but you can foresee enough. If a person can tell you what clubs are hopping on what nights. If a person can tell you what night is wing night, half off drink night, lady's night, and cover charge to get in then it is easy to see he or she is out quite a bit. The problem we face is if the person is very attractive then one tends to overlook all else and commit. It is the things one overlooks early on which leads to the devastation the relationship will face later.

I have shared with others about people who have to have attention is not worth your peace of mind. When a person has to have attention, it will soon bring issues between the two of you. The reason I share this is because as one moves towards committing to a person the narrowing of their desires must happen. If a person who is in the public eye (athlete, actor, politician, and so on) receives a lot of attention from the opposite sex this becomes a mental expectation. The day the well-known person meets someone who catches his or her eye a temporary withdrawal takes place from the attention shown by others. The problem is the withdrawal is temporary and when all of the fantasies conclude the person will return to the streets. Understand, when a person is common to attention from many then one person cannot come close to satisfying that void. Remember this saying:

"The weed of attention is a killer in the garden of life."

I stated within the introduction of this chapter that I will discuss the worker one has become. In the field of buildings or structures, it is common to use words such as, construction or demolition. In relationships people tend to carry out the meaning of these words by the display of their actions. A construction worker will find as many good materials necessary to have the sturdiest structure possible. The worker realizes the strongest materials will provide a sense of security for a long-life expectancy of the structure. There is invested time in this project.

The word demolition is utilized also, but takes a different look within the relationship. Demolition crews come in and salvage anything of value and then destroy the structure. There is no invested time here for all of the damage has been done so the final decisions have been made to demolish the structure.

Relationships work the same way when the truth is told. The possibilities are the sky is the limit when two construction workers meet. Discussions of what is expected, what can go wrong, how to prevent an unforeseen event, and how to handle issues which suddenly arise are taken into consideration. After all, that is what relationships are made of. The two people are on common ground when it comes to goals, family, friends, children, and many more things so talking in the time of crisis becomes easier.

Most relationships are plagued by having one construction worker and one demolition worker. This makes for a troubled life, but not an impossible one. This is where one must find the answers to the reason why the demolition partner destroys. I tell people "people can change, but hanging in there through the transition period is where the frustration develops." The ability to see things positive is the same as to see things negative. The difference is the setting in which one is raised for this is where they learn.

It is the heads constantly bumping which causes the friction the couple suffers. This is amplified by both believing he or she is right based on the backgrounds in which they were raised.

> "To reach the peak of your love two must work together. The day that you do not then you will only enjoy half of your happiness."

These things shared are important for couples who suffer from this torment. It can be through times of trouble that we search our soul and find a way to make it despite the journey traveled.

CHAPTER 10

Maintenance takes two

This chapter will not be as long for this is simple to write about. I am sure many of you have heard the phrase "it takes two" even though this is normally used pertaining to arguments. Well I am going to use this phrase pertaining to the upkeep of relationships on any level. The problems many of us are confronted with is not knowing how to treat the other person or not knowing how to respond when being treated disrespectfully. The thing one should do is layout some ground rules. I know this is not normally initiated by children, but the parents should have created a few for you to follow which you can refer to. The reason much of this is not established within the interactions we have with people is because we have learned the wrong way by default. For example, I will use a couple who have had their first few disagreements and they failed to establish good and thorough communication skills. The parents first teach the child that he or she can talk to them about anything that is troubling. This is a good concept but there is another part to teach…can you guess what that is? I know it is hard because it is so simple that it is overlooked. The child (which is now grown) must be taught that your mate is the person you must now learn to speak with when you are troubled. This is valid for many reasons because it most likely will be with the mate in which your problems exist. Remember I said earlier in the book that when you marry it says, "leaving mother and father and to forsake all others" and that is what it means. In the life one is now adventuring into the problems which will come through life schedules, work schedules, raising children, finances, just plain getting to know one another's difference, and much more that life will throw at you. These issues should not be shared with family and friends for they are the two of your issues to tackle together which is a part of the bonding process. When one of the parties allows a third party to enter the issues within the bond it distorts it, it does not strengthen it. I know many of you have friendships or sibling ties which go way back but I did not make the rules, I am merely introducing or reminding you of the rules. There are rules to life, though not written in every form, but understood through respect and morals. Therefore, I am a huge advocate of learning how to treat others by how you would like to be treated. See, the problem is when we do not understand what it means to interact with each other in a way which consistently shows respect for each other, then things fall around us. What many do not realize is when you run to your friends and family about your relationship drama, you are carrying a one-sided story. Be honest with yourselves about how many people really attempt to convey what the mate was attempting to say. In most cases you were not even listening because you were trying to get in your jabs, rather they were right or wrong. This behavior is what complicates the maintenance the relationship deserves for the two people make-up the problem and everyone else is a hindrance to the healing process. I hope you understand what the last sentence applies. Telling your family and friends about your dramas is like building a snake pit and giving them the poison to bite you when you attempt to cross back over. Let me say that again, as you share with others the drama of your life you are building a pit of venomous snakes which will bite you as you cross back over. Let me give you an illustration. Todd and Tammy are having issues within their relationship. Todd loves the nightlife and it is wearing on Tammy. Tammy remembers she can talk to mom about anything and so she has been sharing the drama with her mother. Now mother has friends and family also so she in turn shares things with them and so on. I hope you are following closely. There has been no wrongdoing on Todd's behalf, but Tammy is just tired of him not being home to help with the house and children. When a person shares with others their perception of the situation but does not share the details, which keeps the story straight, then the listener is left to their own perception of the drama. Now we know how that goes, most everybody comes to the worst scenario possible and this is the poison. This is what one has done, you have built a pit between you and your mate and now in time when you calm down the pit remains. The problem becomes you have filled it with poisonous snakes that now bite you as you attempt to pass back through. You are not hearing me people. Tammy realizes she never stopped loving Todd and behind everyone's backs they have been talking about staying together. First problem here is she needs to sneak around with her own partner for the fear of what the others will say. Tammy brought this on herself. The snakes bite when they see Tammy and Todd together because for some reason, they believe they have a voice. Now they are checking Tammy on her decision to remain with Todd because of his actions. Tammy attempts to regain control of the situation and tells them "you don't know him like I do" and pause. This is true for Tammy had been withholding information which would have given people a better understanding of Tammy's frustration and not Todd's wrongdoing. Yet, if she had talked it out with Todd in the first place this would not be taking place within their relationship. Now do you see how the people outside the relationship can become a hindrance to the healing of the two people that matter. Unfortunately, this happens all the time and to many it is what is considered normal and no-one seeks to change the outcome. I have always attempted to help people understand how to communicate thoroughly and attempt to remain outside of their issues by giving them the information to solve the issues among themselves. Think about this: everybody in the planning process has a say, so if your plan involves more than the two of you then learn to listen to others.

It is important to realize the maintenance is easy when you keep your business between the two of you. If you have never learned then learn this, to hold to your partner, stay cordial to your friends, and keep your family dear for in this one cannot go wrong.

FINAL THOUGHTS

I want all of you readers to understand that I am sharing with you the information in which I compiled throughout the years. I have always had an ability to see outside the box when it comes to life's issues. I hope the things written in this book can and has helped you with the endeavors as well as the issues in your life. I would wish successful relationships for all and the way to make this happen is to have access to information which can put you and keep you on the right path pertaining to the joys of life. Thank you for your support once again.

B. Pollard Sr.

Printed in the United States
By Bookmasters